"Tell me about your father.

"How would you, an adult daughter, respond to that statement? I'm sure many thoughts and feelings about your father rise to the surface. Many may be pleasant; some may be unpleasant.

"Like it or not—your father has made a lasting impression on you. Whether he was close or distant, present or absent, cold or warm, loving or abusive, your father has left his mark on you.

"And your father is still influencing your life today—probably more than you realize."

—H.N.W.

Always DADDY'S Girl

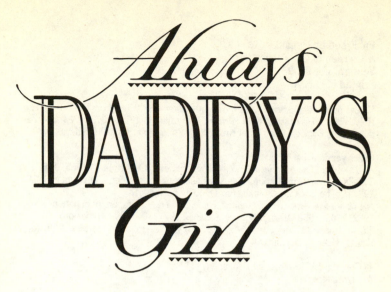

Always DADDY'S Girl

UNDERSTANDING YOUR FATHER'S IMPACT ON WHO YOU ARE

H. Norman Wright

Regal Books
A Division of Gospel Light
Ventura, California, U.S.A.

Published by Regal Books
A Division of GL Publications
Ventura, CA 93006
Printed in U.S.A.

Library of Congress Cataloging-in-Publication Data

Wright, H. Norman.
     Always daddy's girl : understanding your father's impact on who you are / H. Norman Wright.
     p.   cm.
     Includes bibliographical references.
     Hardcover: ISBN 0-8307-1401-4   Paperback: ISBN 0-8307-1354-9
     1. Fathers and daughters. I. Title.
HQ755.85.W73   1989
306.874'2—dc20   89-27319
                                                                      CIP

4 5 6 7 8 9 10 / 93 92 91 90

Rights for publishing this book in other languages are contracted by Gospel Literature International (GLINT) foundation. GLINT also provides technical help for the adaptation, translation, and publishing of Bible study resources and books in scores of languages worldwide. For further information, contact GLINT, Post Office Box 488, Rosemead, California, 91770, U.S.A., or the publisher.

Any omission of credits is unintentional. The publisher requests documentation for future printings.

Contents

ONE

Tell Me About Your Father

"Tell me about your father."

June looked at me with a puzzled expression when I made the request. She was a middle-aged career woman holding a management-level position. "What does my father have to do with why I'm here?" she replied. "I came for counseling because of the difficulties I'm having at my office. My father's been dead for years."

"Tell me about your father."

Lorianne glanced down at the floor defensively, then looked up at me. Tears were welling up in her eyes. "I have difficulty even thinking about my father," she began softly. "I guess I have blocked out many of my experiences with him. I can't remember anything about him before my twelfth birthday. It's funny you would ask me about him. Is there some connection between him and my reasons for coming to see you?" Lorianne had come for counseling because of her continuing pattern of dating men who weren't good for her, as well as a string of broken relationships.

"Tell me about your father."

Jane's eyes brightened with my invitation for her to speak. "Dad was a real winner," she said, smiling. "All of us kids enjoyed our relationship with him as we were growing up. He was fun and easy to talk to, and he didn't withdraw like a lot of men do. I think I appreciated most Dad's belief in me as a woman. Perhaps that's why I feel good about myself as a woman today. He gave me a good sense of security in who I am, not just in what I do. Dad made a lasting impression on me."

Tell me about your father.

How would you, an adult daughter, respond to that statement? I'm sure many thoughts and feelings about your father rise to the surface. Many may be pleasant; some may be unpleasant. Later in this chapter you'll have an opportunity to put them in writing.

What influence has your father been on your life to date? Just as Jane realized her father's impact on her life, so—like it or not—your father has made a lasting impression on you. Whether he was close or distant, present or absent, cold or warm, loving or abusive, your father has left his mark on you.

Your Father and the Men in Your Life

Your father is still influencing your life today—probably more than you realize. For example, your present thoughts and feelings about yourself and your present relationships with other men reflect your father's impact on you. So often, what a father *gives* to his daughter affects her expectations toward the men in her life. Similarly, what a father *withholds* from his daughter can also affect her expectations toward other men.

Michelle came for counseling because of her longing to

be married to a loving, caring husband and have a happy home. She had been looking for a husband for over 20 years. Although she found several men who adored her, she never found her ideal man. She tended to jump quickly into relationships with men who were infatuated with her. But in time she discovered numerous faults in each of them. Michelle fantasized about "Mr. Perfect." Intellectually she knew such a creature didn't exist. But emotionally she was driven to keep looking.

As we talked, Michelle revealed that, as a child, she was her father's favorite—his "pet." He had indulged her and spoiled her in many ways because of the special place Michelle owned in his heart. And in Michelle's eyes, Daddy could do no wrong. But Daddy had only shown Michelle his positive side; she never saw his weaknesses or faults.

How had Michelle's life been influenced by her father for the past 20 years? She had searched in vain for a man who would favor her like Daddy did and who lived as perfectly as Daddy appeared to live. Michelle's father was the model to which she compared all her suitors. As a result, she could not tolerate their normal imperfections and frailties. Michelle had never been able to see past the image of her perfect Daddy to understand that he was just as human as the men she rejected.

I was amazed when another client, I'll call her Karen, described to me the kind of treatment she tolerated from men. She allowed them to mistreat her to the point of cruelty. She wasn't just a pleaser; she was a victim!

"I would like to find just one man who would treat me decently," she said. "I seem to be drawn to men who end up mistreating me, but I don't know why. I'm at the point where I don't want to be hassled by one more man. Never again! I don't even want to try another relationship, but I know I will. What is happening to me?"

During the counseling process, Karen's lack of self-esteem became apparent. She carried deep wounds from the emotional abandonment she experienced as a child. Her parents' relationship was marked by anger and lack of fulfillment. Karen's father had little time for her, controlling her with his anger. There was no physical abuse, but plenty of emotional abuse. She felt worthless and insignificant, especially in her father's eyes.

Karen feels the same way as an adult. She anticipates and expects men to treat her as her father treated her. Karen seems to have an unconscious need to be a victim, which leads her to get involved with men who frighten her and abuse her.

As time went on we discovered that Karen's abusive relationships with men met another need in her life. Her poor relationship with her father left her aching with sadness, depression, anger and bitterness. These feelings were difficult to face. But when she was involved with an abusive partner, her inner pain was temporarily obliterated. She had to use all her emotional energy to survive her current relationship. The pain of the present became a shield against the pain in the past.

I realize that Karen's situation may sound strange. But many women today suffer similar problems due to the powerful negative impact their fathers have made in their lives.

Denise came to see me totally frustrated with her husband. She described him as a likable man, but passive and ineffective. She admitted that she had been trying to change him for ten years, to no avail.

As we talked, Denise eventually told me about her father, who was also likable, but "wishy-washy." He had tremendous ability and potential, but he was never successful. Denise's mother criticized him and ran him down constantly. Denise felt at times as though she needed to support and protect her father. She couldn't understand why he failed to achieve, but she never stopped believing in him.

There are multitudes of women whose marriages suffer under the painful influence of their relationships with their fathers.

Denise was drawn to her husband by qualities which were similar to her father's. She entered the marriage believing that she would be able to stimulate and encourage him to do wonderful things. It didn't work, but she kept trying. Why did Denise choose a man so similar to her wishy-washy father? She wanted to succeed where her mother had failed. She wanted to prove by her efforts with her husband that her father *was* inherently a successful man. Her father *could have* achieved if he had had the right woman.

Denise's case may sound unusual, but it's certainly not isolated. There are multitudes of women whose marriages suffer under the painful influence of their relationships with their fathers.

Your Father's Influence

If you were to describe your relationship with your father, what would you say? How has your relationship with your father affected your relationships with men, your career and your feelings about yourself? Take several minutes to evaluate your past and/or present relationship with your father by answering the following 11 questions:

1. What do you feel are/were your father's positive qualities?

2. What do you feel are/were your father's negative qualities?

3. How did you feel about your father as a child through age ten?

   From age 11-20?

   From age 21-30?

   At the present time?

4. What emotions did your father express openly? How did he express them?

5. Describe how you and your father communicate(d).

6. What was the most pleasant experience you had with your father?

7. What was the most unpleasant experience you had with your father?

8. What is/was your father's goal in life?

9. In what ways are you like your father?

10. In what ways are you different from your father?

11. How do you feel your father influenced your choice of a man (men)?

The first two questions are among the most revealing of your father's influence on your life. Over the years of my counseling practice, I have asked these questions to hundreds of women in their 20s and 30s. Perhaps some of the answers I have received will give you added insight into your relationship with your father and the men in your life. In subsequent chapters we will discuss many of the topics suggested in questions 3-11. But for now, read carefully the influential positive and negative qualities women have identified in their fathers:

Positive Qualities

He's affectionate. He is generous, kind, loving, likes to have fun, likes to be with family. He loves the Lord, works hard. He is intelligent, supportive, thinks about what is best for the family.

He is honest, very friendly, knowledgeable, intelligent, dependable, trustworthy, always learning, up on current events, a hard worker.

My father was a very loving man. He readily showed his feeling of love to us. He was also very hard-working—always kept himself busy. He was also a very dedicated Christian.

Strength of character, respectable, leader, athletically fit, loyal, hard-working.

My dad is real achievement-oriented. I haven't decided if that is positive or negative. At one time he was juggling three things at once. When I was growing up I never saw him, which I consider a negative since he missed out on about ten years of my growing up. I don't feel like I know my father real well and I can't really think of positive or negative qualities. He's not very excitable. He'll try anything. He has his opinion and that's the way it is.

My father is self-disciplined, responsible. He has grown to show his deep feelings of love for family. He tries to be more understanding and allow for two-way thought and conversation. Family priorities are first—home, education, recreation, spiritual. He is handsome and well-respected.

He is a self-starter, will tackle any new experience, hobby or recreation even though he may not have the necessary skills. He loves my mother. He displays great loyalty to his wife and sister. His emotions run deep, and he displays admirable professional self-improvement abilities. He is stable and consistent. He likes to be teased and to tease his daughters. He has learned to play well and I admire his learning ability. He is honest, kind and generous. He copes well. He is capable of change and lets go of the past well.

Compassionate, goal-oriented, tender, godly, loving, communicative, understanding, gentle, loving, a figure-outer of things.

My father has a lot of patience and endurance. He always keeps busy and accomplishes what he starts. He is the authority figure in our home. He has many responsibilities and fulfils them all. Good sense of humor.

He's had clear goals for himself and his family. He has worked to achieve these goals. He is kind-hearted, takes groceries to the needy (usually elderly) and "forgotten ones" in his community (this was not public knowledge!). He loves his family dearly. He is wise and caring. He has given job opportunities to young and old, helping them develop their self-worth and achieve their goals. Many come to him for counsel on personal and business matters.

My dad is a kind, loving, understanding person. He is considerate and easy to talk to. He is friendly and warm toward others.

He is kind and very supportive of me. I feel very accepted by him. I respect him as an intelligent man who works hard, and I am proud of him. He's generous, even-tempered. He is stable, loving and pleasant to be around.

Before the divorce, he would always listen to me when I needed to talk. He was very supportive and encouraging. He set aside time to be with me, include me in his activities and make me feel special. He was like my best friend, readily showing affection when I needed it. He is very sensitive and stable, and has a sense of humor.

My father is gentle, sensitive, kind, humble, loving, intelligent (knowledgeable), caring, a good listener, spiritually sound, a lot of wisdom, fair, easy-going, patient.

Very giving, extremely interested in children, easy-going. He remains calm in anxiety-producing situations. He's easy to get along with, goes along with most things, encourages and supports—just always himself!

My father is in control of his life, family, employees, etc. Strong, authoritative man—not easily taken advantage of. Organized, knows what he wants from life, and therefore is decisive.

My dad is a very caring man. He has always been there for me as a support and model. He was always willing to lend a hand, and help lighten any load. My dad is very gentle. He rarely raises his voice. My dad is very good with people. He reaches out and makes people feel very accepted and comfortable.

My father has always been a provider of material things and finances. He has always been there. After the divorce, my father kept his relationship open to his kids. He did not allow the divorce to affect his relationship with me.

My father was a good provider for his family, a faithful husband, and supportive of us, although he had trouble expressing his support. He was always willing to participate in our activities as best he could, usually as a spectator.

Negative Qualities

He was not a good listener. Sometimes too much of a Pollyanna, avoiding conflict. He was not disciplined physically.

He does not communicate at all. He is not sensitive to his wife's needs. He does not understand the emotional side of people very well. He doesn't strive for quality in his work.

Stubborn, interpersonally immature, intimate with relatives, but still a loner. Sometimes he has tunnel-vision, impulsive, emotionally distant.

He wasn't very good at money management.

Because my father did not communicate well I was never able to talk to him about what was happening in my life, so we have not been close.

He has a bad temper at times and yells sometimes. The television seems to dominate his life at home. He is a new Christian, but not very interested in growing or reading the Scriptures at this time.

Drinks too much, tries to manipulate me and my decisions, holds onto the past. Doesn't care about himself, is not a Christian. Bad temper, worries too much about money, negative about life. Won't show affection or loving emotion, won't ever cry. Has difficulty being honest, doesn't trust people—especially women. Resents my mother.

He is quick-tempered, isolational and sometimes violent. He doesn't accept responsibility for the bad things he has done. He doesn't understand people's feelings or how to deal with people. He has never grown up. He still has temper tantrums like a child.

He is a successful workaholic. He is controlling, verbally abusive and thinks I am a failure. Success is everything, materialism is everything. He thinks negatively and brings people down. He isn't emotional or loving.

Gives conditional support. Used Mother as total communication mediator. Somewhat intimidating, cold, closed off to any subject which might disappoint him, challenge his beliefs or hurt him. Critical.

My father never has been a nurturer of my emotional needs. Because of this, I've never been as close as I desire to be to him.

Controlling. He is stubborn and bull-headed. He is repetitive. He appears to consider himself and no one else at times. He was mean, almost brutal, to my sister until she left home. He does not really "know" my mother. Or if he does, he has chosen to avoid her by working day and night, not making time for her. As a result, 44 years later there is a rift and sadness between them which almost cannot be bridged. He consistently lets his feelings of wanting to be boss get in the way of enjoying joint family projects. I don't want that kind of partner.

He has a short temper; holds grudges. If someone gets on his bad side, that's where they stay! Thank goodness you have a better chance of measuring up if you're in the family. He is intense; never tired. I think he even works taking a vacation.

Doesn't seem to know how to communicate feelings or admit to and deal with relational problems. Although he doesn't lose his temper, he can become passively aggressive or stubborn.

Impatient, strict, lack of sensitivity. Doesn't express his feelings or emotions very well. Has a short temper about certain issues. Very demanding of people. Doesn't always think before he says things.

My father never has been a nurturer of my emotional needs. Because of this, I've never been as close as I desire to be to him. He also doesn't credit me for my growth as a person, but cuts me down or ignores me.

Non-communicative, not readily sharing his emotions. Uses silence to hurt others. Stubborn. Not spontaneous. Very much of a rut person. Does not confront conflicts. Would prefer to ignore them than face them, even if confrontation would solve the problem.

Failure to keep his obligations and commitments. Got angry and kept it to himself. Wouldn't let himself come close to others.

Lacks common sense sometimes. Unmotivated. Goes off into his own little world sometimes. Over-protective.

Slightly anti-social, overly dependent on my mother. Doesn't do his share of work around the house. Critical at times, poor listener, sometimes negative. Not too forgiving, holds grudges against in-laws. Speaks before thinking sometimes.

Before you continue in the book, read through these two lists again. Underline each word or phrase which represents the positive and negative qualities you see in your own father. You may want to reflect on your perceptions of him at three stages of your life: when you were a child, an adolescent, or now as an adult. If your father is deceased, evaluate his qualities through your last memories of him. This exercise will assist you in discovering and dealing with your father's influence on you.

Father's Values, Your Values

Your father imparted, or at least attempted to impart, some values to you. Do you know what those values are? Do you remember your father's beliefs in certain areas of life? Spend a few minutes reflecting on how your father's values have impacted your life. Listed below are several important life issues. Think carefully about what your dad believed about each issue. Then complete the statement which begins "My dad always said" as it pertains to each issue. Notice that two examples are given for each topic.

Then complete the statement which begins "What I believe now is" by summarizing your position on each issue. Compare the two statements to see how your values and beliefs parallel your father's:

WHAT DAD AND I BELIEVE

Money

Examples: Dad always said, "Don't waste your money on trivial items."
Dad always said, "Money doesn't grow on trees."

My dad always said, —————————————.

What I believe now is, —————————————.

Food

Examples: Dad always said, "Be sure you eat the right foods."
Dad always said, "You eat all that and you will really be fat."

My dad always said, —————————————.

What I believe now is, —————————————.

Sex

Examples: Dad always said, "Sex is a gift from God. But it has its place only in marriage."
Dad always said, "Watch out so you don't get into trouble by the way you dress."

My dad always said, —————————————.

What I believe now is, —————————————.

Women

Examples: Dad always said, "Women are too emotional and flighty."
Dad always said, "Women are here for one purpose."

My dad always said, —————————————.

What I believe now is, _____.

Christianity

Examples: Dad always said, "Your faith in Christ is your most important decision in life."
Dad always said, "The values of our faith are very hard to live up to."

My dad always said, _____.

What I believe now is, _____.

Leisure

Examples: Dad always said, "Be sure you use your time wisely.
Dad always said, "Relax and have fun. When you're an adult, you'll have to work."

My dad always said, _____.

What I believe now is, _____.

Work

Examples: Dad always said, "You're not old enough to have a job yet."
Dad always said, "Work hard in every job you have and you'll get ahead."

My dad always said, _____.

What I believe now is, _____.

Men

Examples: Dad always said, "Watch out when you date. Men only want one thing."
Dad always said, "Find a man with brains and money rather than looks."

My dad always said, _____.

What I believe now is, _____.

School

Examples: Dad always said, "Do your best and bring home *A*'s and I'll be proud of you."
Dad always said, "Why should a girl go to college? It's a waste of time and money."

My dad always said, _____.

What I believe now is, _____.

Vocation

Examples: Dad always said, "You'd make a good teacher."
Dad always said, "You will end up being a doctor."

My dad always said, _____.

What I believe now is, _____.

Self-esteem

Examples: Dad always said, "Watch out that you don't get too impressed with yourself."
Dad always said, "I wasn't much good."

My dad always said, _____.

What I believe now is, _____.

My Friends

Examples: Dad always said, "I selected good friends."
Dad always said, "I spent too much time with my friends when I was a teen."

My dad always said, _____.

What I believe now is, _____.

Fears

Examples: Dad always said, "There is nothing to be afraid of in this world."
Dad always said, "I'm afraid you won't turn out like Mom and I want."

My dad always said, _____.

What I believe now is, _____.

Emotions

Examples: Dad always said, "Emotions and feelings are a waste of time. They get you into trouble."
Dad always said, "I don't understand your feelings most of the time."

My dad always said, —————————————.

What I believe now is, —————————————.

What have you learned about you and your father? Perhaps you can share some of your insights with him. He may be surprised that you remember what he believes.

In this chapter you have remembered and expressed a lot about your father. You've already taken a giant step toward understanding and responding to his influence in your life. The next step is to investigate the images daughters carry of their fathers. What was/is your father like? Does he match the ideal of the perfect father? Read on.

TWO

Images of Your Father

Father. The word evokes many images in a daughter's mind. He's called Father, Dad, Daddy, Pa, Papa and Pop. To the chagrin of many mothers, an infant daughter's first word is often "Dada" instead of "Mama."

A father enters a little girl's world wearing several hats. She often perceives him as the director of her life, her mentor and her guide. She may see him as her provider and the source of her security. Many young girls grow up hearing the comforting words, "When Daddy gets home, he'll fix it." You may have memories of a daddy who could solve every problem and unscramble even the worst messes.

Perhaps you grew up in a fairly traditional home where your father was the primary source of income. He paid the bills and awarded allowances on payday. He took the family on vacations, and when you went to the restaurant, he ordered for everybody. In your youthful innocence, you saw your father as all-powerful. Daughters like the feeling of safety and strength this image conveys.

Your image of your father may include the scriptural characteristics of a family leader, such as the description of a godly man in 1 Timothy 3:4: "He must manage his own family well and see that his children obey him with proper respect." Perhaps he was a good example of such biblical guidelines for fathering as: "These commandments that I give you today are to be upon your hearts. Impress them on your children. Talk about them when you sit at home and when you walk along the road, when you lie down and when you get up" (Deut. 6:6-7); "Fathers, do not exasperate your children; instead, bring them up in the training and instruction of the Lord" (Eph. 6:4); and "Fathers, do not embitter your children, or they will become discouraged" (Col. 3:21). Fathering is a high spiritual calling. Fathers are to teach, encourage, guide and provide for their children. If your father filled the role of the spiritual leader in your home, you are blessed and should be deeply thankful.

Up until now we have been talking about fathers who have left a positive image in their adult daughters. But maybe you can't fully relate to the picture of the strong, loving, godly family leader and provider because you didn't have that kind of father. Your father might have been more like the fathers of Sleeping Beauty and Cinderella, who affected their daughters' lives in ways which were not all positive.

Sleeping beauty's father was also the king. He loved his daughter, but unfortunately he forgot to invite one of the oldest and most powerful fairies in his kingdom to the girl's christening. His oversight resulted in 100 years of sleep and inactivity for his daughter.

Cinderella's father created problems for his daughter

too. He allowed himself to be dominated by a strong, overbearing second wife. Because of this, Cinderella was condemned by her stepmother to live in rags and serve the household as the maid.

In both fairy tales, the fathers were present in their daughters' lives, but ineffective. The glory of each story is that both girls were rescued from the dungeons of their parental homes by handsome young princes. Similarly, many women today who were raised in homes governed by less than ideal fathers latched onto the first available "prince" who proposed to them, hoping to find the safety and security which was lacking in their fathers.[1]

It's also possible that the image you carry is not of an ideal father or a present but ineffective father, but of an abusive or absent father. Perhaps your memories of your father are so darkly clouded by his negative qualities that you struggle to find within yourself many positive thoughts or feelings about him. No matter what your image of your father may be, the following chapters will help you deal with your past experiences and present situation in a meaningful and productive way.

A Father's Unique Contribution

Fathers have a unique and definite role in shaping the future of their children. Willard Gaylin, author of *Feelings*, describes it:

> If we experience something too strongly in the past, we may anticipate it where we ought not and perceive it where it does not exist. If, for example, we were intimidated by a punitive father who terrified us, we may approach all authority figures with the bias of that early dominate memory. The memory of

that authority may possess a greater reality to us than the actual authority figure with whom we were involved. Regardless of how gentle and unchallenging the authority figure is, we may approach each teacher, each employer as though he had both the power and the personality of that dominant father who once ruled our life.[2]

In her extensive interviews with women, Suzanne Fields identified some important issues in the father's influence in his daughter's life:

As adult women describe their memories, they touch on the key issues of adult sexual and psychological maturity. Women see father-daughter parallels in their marriages and love relationships as father casts a lengthening shadow over sexuality, work, procreation and recreation.

Competency and *Femininity* are the twin values most of the women I interviewed stressed as the values strongly influenced by their father, the positive qualities that feed their self-esteem, their work, and love.[3]

Your parents were your first models, and each parent played a different role in your development. To be sure, the roles of mother and father overlapped in many areas of your upbringing and development. Let's look specifically at some areas where your father's contribution stands apart from your mother's role.

Introduction to masculinity. Your father was the vehicle for introducing you to the opposite sex. How carefully you were taught about masculinity—both directly and indirectly—by your father, and how well you learned those lessons, will be evident in your interaction with the men in your personal and business life. Your father has colored your perception of men and shaped your expectations of how men will or should behave toward you.

A father's love. Mothers and fathers express their love for their daughters in different ways. A mother's love tends to be unconditional, providing a general sense of security. But a father's love is often given as a reward for his daughter's performance, causing a daughter to assume that his love must be earned.

The expression of a father's love is further complicated by the fact that many fathers are unable to offer spontaneous, direct affection to their daughters. They tend to hide their tender emotions. Mothers often must translate for their daughters the unexpressed love of fathers. "Your father really loves you," a mother will console her daughter, "but he just doesn't show it openly." A daughter who is fortunate enough to have a father capable of expressing his deepest feelings has been given a precious gift which will enrich her life and her memories of her father.

What about you? How did your father share his love with you, especially his tender emotions? Was your mother involved in translating his love into terms you could understand?

"That's my girl." The validation and approval a father gives his daughter in her early years is different from that given by her mother. Mother is usually around much more than father, so his comments and responses often have more impact. Why? Because they are expressed differently and less frequently. His positive involvement can help keep his daughter from becoming overly dependent on her mother.

A father's confidence in his daughter and her capabilities will instill in her the confidence to survive on her own.

It is important that a father respect, admire and, above all, take seriously the fact that his little girl is in the process of becoming a woman. If a father does not let go of his "little girl" at some point, an unhealthy psychological dependence may develop. When an overdependency persists after the daughter reaches adulthood, the two will continue to respond to each other as parent and child instead of moving to the level of relating to each other as adults. Your father may always be an authority figure in your life in some ways, but he should not be as authoritarian in your adult life as he was when you were a child.

Fathers play a crucial role in their daughters' perception of ambition, achievement and competence. A wise father will convey that none of these characteristics are incompatible with femininity.

Shaping the future. Fathers have a unique way of introducing their daughters to the future and shaping their roles. Some fathers instill in their daughters an *expanded* view of their potential, as illustrated by the comments of a successful business woman I talked with recently. "When I was very young," she said, "my father would sit me on his knee and tell me there wasn't anything I couldn't do. I could accomplish anything I chose to attempt. He gave me a belief in myself and my abilities."

Sadly, other fathers allow their daughters only a *limited* view of their role in the world. They communicate that women must follow the prescribed roles of wife, mother, housekeeper, volunteer, etc. These are excellent roles as long as they are a daughter's choice from among a variety of options for women today. But many daughters are not encouraged to be all they could be. And many women, who succeed outside the home despite their fathers' narrow views, are afraid of too much success. They project the perspectives from their fathers onto the men in their lives, fearing a loss of popularity among their male co-workers and the possibility of becoming a threat to their husbands.

Fathers play a crucial role in their daughters' perception of ambition, achievement and competence. A wise father will convey that none of these characteristics are incompatible with femininity. Women also learn about power in work relationships from their fathers. They can learn about the positive side and the limitations of the traditional male approach to work. Hopefully they will also learn the futility of attempting to achieve too much and of building their identity upon achievement.

The Feminine Factor

Your relationship with your father was your critical initial interaction with the masculine gender. He was the first man whose attention you wanted to gain. He was the first man you flirted with, the first man to cuddle you and kiss you, the first man to prize you as a very special girl among all other girls. All of these experiences with your father were vital to the nurturing of the element which makes you different from him and all other men: your femininity. The fawning attention of a father for his daughter prepares her for her uniquely feminine role as a girlfriend, fiance and wife.

If there was something lacking in your relationship with your father when you were a child, the development of your femininity suffered the most. Why? As a little girl, you by nature expressed all the budding traits of the feminine gender. If your father was emotionally or physically absent, or was harsh, rejecting or angry toward you, you automatically and subconsciously attached his disapproval to your femininity. You didn't have the intellectual capacity to understand his rejection, nor did you have the inner defensive structure to insulate yourself against it. You simply and naively reasoned, "I want Daddy to like me; Daddy doesn't like me the way I am; I will change the way I am so Daddy will like me."

When a father does not value or respond to his daughter's femininity, she is stunted in her development. When a daughter has little experience in delighting her father as a child, she is incomplete. She is left to discover her femininity for herself, often with tragic results in her relationships with men.

Fathers do affect their daughters' femininity. A father who is not too threatened by his daughter's sexuality and who is warm and accepting toward her, helps her grow into womanhood in a normal manner. It's true that a woman's sexuality develops over her entire lifetime, but it is definitely encouraged—or retarded—by her early interactions with her father. Her femininity is encouraged by his smile or wink when she bats her eyelashes at him, and by his expression of enjoyment for her hair style, new dress or new shoes.

Do you remember the excitement of getting a new outfit and looking forward to your father's response? Did you hope he would be happy and tell you how pretty you looked? Did he pick you up and twirl you around? A woman's sexual self-image is partially molded by her father's responses to her.[4]

Leon Hammer, a psychotherapist who deals with sexual unresponsiveness in women, discusses the father's role in developing his daughter's sexuality:

> This man must see, feel, appreciate and respond to every aspect of the little girl's femininity—her hair, her body, her clothes, her laughter, her voice, her walk, her gestures. He must show his pleasure by holding her, kissing her, tickling her, cuddling her, and playing with her. The pleasure he gets and the pleasure he gives in open response will determine how far the little girl can be pleased by the presence and existence of a man.[5]

When a girl grows to womanhood without the benefits of her femininity being affirmed by her father, she may become, as one writer described, an "armored Amazon." She reacts against her negligent father by assuming some of the masculine functions of fathering. Since Daddy didn't provide the masculine image she needed, she decides to fill that role herself. She builds up a strong, masculine self-identity through personal achievements or by aggressively fighting for a cause. She may reflect fathering traits by taking control of people and situations and "laying down the law." She's a human dynamo at work, and at home she runs the family like a business.

This pseudo-masculinity serves as the woman's protective shell. It is her armor and shield against the pain of being abandoned or rejected by her father. She uses her armor to protect her soft, vulnerable feminine side which was rejected instead of affirmed by her father. But the armor which effectively keeps the outside from getting in also keeps the inside from getting out. The armored Amazon has difficulty showing her feminine feelings, the naturally soft side of her life. She alienates herself from healthy relationships with men and from the full life she was created to enjoy as a woman.[6]

Do you identify at all with this description? Can you see some traits of the armored Amazon in your personality? Are you suddenly aware that your life today reflects your father's denial of your femininity as a child? Keep reading. The chapters ahead will help you come to terms with yourself and your feelings about your father.

The Affirming Father

One of the most important contributions a father can make to his growing daughter's life is his affirmation of her. If your father modeled some of the characteristics of the affirming father discussed in these next pages, chances are you have a good relationship with him (if he is alive), a positive self-image and healthy relationships with the men in your life. If your father did not match up to the profile described here, you probably have difficulty getting along with him now. Depending on the level of deprivation you experienced, you may also have trouble accepting yourself and relating to other men.

As you compare your father to the characteristics below, be careful not to condemn him, or pity yourself, for his failures. The purpose of this section is to help you understand how your father's behavior has shaped your life and to pave the way for your relationship with him to improve.

A balanced approach. It is important for a father to affirm his daughter's physical qualities, but not to minimize other qualities such as achievements, values and attitudes, especially those which are taught in Scripture. A daughter needs love and approval exactly as she is, not for what her father wishes she were. Compliments and affirmations should be expressed frequently and unconditionally. I've heard fathers say to their daughters, "If you don't take better care of your appearance, no one will want to ask you out," or, "If you don't lose some weight, you can forget about any boys coming around here." Comments like these, even if they contain a kernel of truth, are the opposite of affirmation. The father's standards for what the girl ought to be are obviously more important than what she is, cutting deeply into a girl's feelings.

How did your father affirm you? Was there a balance of comments, or did he focus too much on your physical appearance? Was his affirmation unconditional or based on your compliance with his standards for you?

A focus on the feminine. Some fathers encourage the feminine side of their daughters, but others are threatened by it. They don't know how to handle a little girl's adoration, so they retreat from her feminine responses. This rebuff from her father may cause a daughter to feel uncomfortable in future relationships with men, since her initial "courtship" experience with her father was unrewarding.

Some fathers may have other motives for affirming the femininity of their daughters, as related by William Woolfolk and Donna W. Cross:

> Fathers who are very strong or dominant can influence their daughters in a major way. In fact some of them may shape their daughter's character as a compensation for not having the kind of mother or wife they wanted. For some fathers, their daughters

become a hope for their future. Their daughters are someone they can mold into the kind of person that will bring them the kind of happiness they never had. A father's influence is conveyed so indirectly that many have underrated the extent of their influence over the years. Dad is the vehicle through which she arrives at her understanding of her value. William Reynolds in *The American Father* said that neither "wife, son, mother, father, lover (nor) mistress can give Dad what his daughter can: approval and admiration for the doing of absolutely nothing." Father's girl can invest him with the robes of the true hero, and the sole *quid pro quo* is that he merely show up. Everywhere else father goes he has to earn his way for love, respect, money, or whatever. Only his daughter gives her rewards to him for free.[7]

A father who is able to admire his daughter's dresses, her initial efforts at makeup, her jewelry and her attractiveness as a female helps her develop the confidence she needs for relating to other men later on. Unfortunately, some fathers are so uncomfortable with their daughter's attempts at femininity that they ridicule them instead of affirm them. They tend to be absent when she displays her charms, or they push her away by being too tired or too irritable to respond affirmatively. The results of these rejections will be seen in a young woman's insecurity and doubt about her ability to attract a man.

Did your father appreciate and affirm your femininity, or was he uncomfortable with it? Can you see how his responses to your femininity have shaped your life today?

Affirming the whole person. Genuine affirmation is important not only for the momentary feeling of security it provides, but because it opens the gateway to healthy future relationships. It is from her father that a girl needs to know that she is attractive, that her conversation is interesting and that her creativity is worthwhile. If her father applauds her mental and spiritual attributes during her formative years, she will learn not to rely solely on shallow qualities like sex appeal to attract men as an adult. Affirmation from her father in proper doses will convince her that she is an important person, not a sex object.

If her father is perceptive, he will begin early in his daughter's life to let her know how pleased he is with her as a person. He will affirm her for being, not just doing. He will urge her to copy the admirable traits in her mother. Through approval and affirmation he will constantly highlight her developing capacities. He will point out the achievements of other women who are accomplishing things in the world, and he will encourage her to make worthwhile accomplishments of her own. As she learns to please him in these ways, she will be able to handle herself with confidence among other men as she grows older. Her adult relationships with men will be of an extremely high caliber if her father allows her to have a high caliber relationship with himself.[8]

The Wounding Father

It would be wonderful if more fathers were able to affirm their daughters this way. But because of background, personal experiences or lack of opportunity or choice to grow, many fathers end up wounding their daughters instead of nurturing them through affirmation. Some fathers who are weak in character, or who flit from job to job, or who are consumed by alcohol, or who are compulsive gamblers are a source of shame for their daughters. I have met them. A father may wound his daughter by being absent, either through divorce, illness, death or uninvolvement. He may also wound her by failing to set limits for her and by ignoring scriptural guidelines for his life. He may indulge her so much that she never develops boundaries, values or respect for authority in her life.

Some fathers may unconsciously fall in love with their daughters and in some way keep them as personal prisoners. Some men are biased and macho-masculine, thriving on power and authority, looking down on their daughters and devaluing their feminine characteristics and qualities. Some men work 80 hours a week and are highly successful, but wound their daughters by being passive and detached at home. A father needs to be there for his daughter physically, emotionally, intellectually and spiritually. By committing himself to be an affirming father, he can help his daughter develop in all these dimensions as well.[9]

Many women have been wounded by their fathers because of a lack of acceptance, creating feelings of insecurity, detachment and isolation. As a result, these women do not know how to be close to any man. Some of them learn not to expect love, warmth, closeness or intimacy from a man because these qualities were never evident in their fathers. Often these women who have been deprived of fatherly love and attention feel cheated. They smolder with deep-seated anger toward their fathers and men in general. When any other man lets her down, her pent up anger erupts. Many men are punished and driven away from these women, not for what they have done, but for what wounding fathers did earlier in their daughters' lives.

Some wounded women react to their deprivation of fatherly love in the opposite way: displaying an excessive appetite for men. They demand relationships with men which are marked by total devotion. I've met some wounded women who want to live in a perpetual state of courtship excitement. When a relationship becomes routine or predictable, she ends it and seeks another man who will satisfy her craving for intense love and acceptance.

Does your image of your father contain some of the characteristics of the wounding father described here? Do you identify with the traits of the wounded woman? The good news is that your wounds, and your relationship with your wounding father, can be healed.

The Challenge of Adolescence

A father's influence on his daughter's life is critical in her childhood years. But what effect does a father have on his daughter when she hits the adolescent years? He still has a significant influence. The young woman is beginning the process of emotional separation from her father. This fact in itself brings a certain amount of pain and upset to the father-daughter relationship, even when that relationship is positive.

A father can handicap his adolescent daughter emotionally and sexually at this time by responding negatively to her developing sexuality. As a girl's body begins to mature, many fathers unconsciously withdraw from their daughters. Fathers are sometimes bothered by the sexual effect their daughters have on them or the effect they may have on their daughters. As a result, lap-sitting, kissing and hugging tend to decline.

But teenaged girls still need contact with their fathers. Certain types of horseplay may no longer be appropriate, but physical affection can still be expressed in nonsexual ways. Girls who become promiscuous in adolescence often come from homes where fathers have not been

affectionate. These fathers failed to meet their daughters'
needs to be touched and physically affirmed.

When a father retreats or withdraws from his daughter
because he is threatened by her physical development, he
abandons much of his parental role of counseling and interaction solely to her mother. Also, his withdrawal at this
time leaves the girl ill-equipped to respond adequately to
men romantically. Dr. William S. Appleton says:

> It is the fortunate adolescent girl who has a warm,
> not seductive, and attentive, not interfering, father
> who brings reasonable patience to bear upon her
> rebellion and aggression. When she is fourteen or fif-
> teen she can shout at him, "I hate you" and he will
> not retaliate too angrily or withdraw from her. They
> both try as well as they can to adjust to her becoming
> a sexual woman, rather than pretending she is still a
> little girl. He enjoys seeing her body mature without
> comment or fear. As he accepts her sexual develop-
> ment, so will she, although both are a little uncomfor-
> table about it. Parental responsiveness and accep-
> tance help a woman to grow sexually. By trying not
> to rival her boyfriends, not to be brighter and more
> attractive than they, but to act the part of father even
> when it requires stands which are unpopular with her
> and make her angry, he allows someone to take her
> away from him.[10]

A daughter's maturing into adolescence is a problem
mainly for the father. Separation is imminent, and that's
uncomfortable for him. Because of his anxiety, any problems which developed between father and daughter during
her childhood may be perpetuated and reinforced during
her teen years. The fact that his little girl will soon be leav-

ing home vividly underscores the reality of his aging process—and that's *very* uncomfortable for him!

A daughter's teen years are also a problem for a father because they coincide with his other mid-life struggles with his job, marriage, etc. She may become embarrassed at the smallest thing he does or says, thus straining the relationship. He wants predictability from his daughter, but she is more unpredictable than ever. He wants to hold onto her, but he knows he must release her from childhood to become a more independent "semi-adult." Yet letting her become independent, and not need him as much, leaves a void in his life.

What a difference it would make in a family if a father could talk about his feelings of discomfort and change with his wife and daughter during this time. But very few fathers do. If a family was able to work through these changes together, everyone involved would be more comfortable.

Another major adjustment for a father during his daughter's teen years is when boys begin hanging around the house or when he hears cracking baritone voices on the telephone asking for her. Fathers may feel unsettled at the invasion of boys because they feel it is happening too soon—even though they know it is inevitable. It's a sign that he's losing his little girl. He may feel helpless, jealous, protective or lonely—or all of the above!

An authoritarian father may bear down during his daughter's teen years, controlling her in order to block the development of the independence she needs to move into adulthood. Many fathers want their daughters to be independent—but only according to their rules. His excuse is, "I only have her best interests at heart. And since I'm older and wiser, I think I know what's best for her."

A passive father may tend to withdraw even more at this time. His hurts—including feelings of being betrayed by his daughter—are not expressed verbally, but rather through his behavior. A teenaged daughter needs her father, however. If he retreats emotionally, she may feel abandoned and even guilty that she is responsible. As one writer so beautifully states, "For a young girl to move into adulthood as a woman a father must allow himself to grieve the loss of his little girl in order to celebrate the arrival of a young woman."[11]

During his daughter's adolescence, a father feels displaced. She used to ask dad how he liked her hair; now she asks her boyfriend. These and other behaviors cause some fathers to feel shut out of their daughters' lives. And often they are puzzled by her strange new behavior. Her emotions flow up, down and sideways; her little-girl predictability is no more. Fathers need to be patient and understanding during this transition. Dad must accept the fact that he is no longer the most important male in his daughter's life. His love and approval, however, are still very important to her.[12]

One of the ways a father can prepare his daughter for young womanhood and the challenges of relating to boys is by sharing with her some of his own insights about men and how they respond to women. Unfortunately, few fathers take this opportunity. They characteristically overstate the advice, "Be careful and don't get into trouble with boys." This response often reflects a father's anxiety about his daughter's developing sexuality. His anxiety may also reflect the way he behaved during his teen years.

But the father who gives his daughter insight about the ways boys think about girls, about the peer pressure boys face to perform sexually and about how to anticipate some of the boy-girl situations she will encounter, will help her handle the rough times of adolescence. He can assure her in advance, and reassure her in the moments she faces disappointments with the boys in her life, that her worth is not based on the responses of others. He must assure her that her pain and hurt are normal. If a father helps prepare his daughter in advance for the challenges of her teen years, and listens to her in the midst of them, she will probably turn to him in times of despair knowing that he is available to her.

It is vital for his daughter's development that a father encourage her transition into the career world and accept her departure from the home.

I remember numerous times when my daughter, Sheryl, approached me during her junior and senior high years with problems. Since I tend to give advice and seek solutions (typical traits of a male and a teacher!), I learned to ask her, "Do you want me to just listen or do you want some suggestions?" Most of the time she answered, "I'd like some suggestions," but there were a number of times when all she needed was a listening ear. I must admit that just listening wasn't always the easiest thing for me to do!

What do you remember about your father's involvement with you during adolescence? Was he authoritarian or passive concerning your sexual development and your early involvement with boys? Was he approachable or aloof when it came to discussing problems of adolescence?

When Daughter Leaves the Nest

When daughters become adults, some fathers know how to let them go, but others continue to hang on. It is vital for his daughter's development that a father encourage her transition into the career world and accept her departure from the home. This doesn't mean he disappears from her life. His continuing availability is also important—and that's the key word: *availability*. The adult daughter has the option—no longer the responsibility—to draw upon her father as a resource.

The daughter's transition to adulthood often carries with it a sense of sadness for her father. But if he can mourn, accept the loss and recover, he will move on into a new and equally enjoyable phase of relationship with his adult daughter.

The way in which a daughter separates from her father will color the way she relates to other men in her life. The daughter who experiences rejection by her father, or who perceives her father's exit from her life as rejection, may develop anger and anxiety toward men in general. The fear of future rejection by men will build hostility, which increases the likelihood that other men *will* reject her. The daughter who interprets her father's divorce from her mother as a rejection of her may live in continual fear of being rejected by her husband some day. Unfortunately, the way a fearful daughter responds to her husband may end up bringing about the very separation she fears. If her husband behaves at all like her father, she may be reminded of the disappointments she experienced as a child and she may overreact to her husband.

Fathers usually give gifts to their daughters. Many of them are expensive, chosen with care. But some material gifts are given as a substitute for the gifts of love and time which a daughter needs from her father more than she needs jewelry, a car or a college education. The best gift a father can give his departing daughter is his support and belief in her—a belief which will encourage her to develop to her fullest potential as a person and as a woman. Hopefully, this gift will include introducing her in a healthy way to the love of her heavenly Father and His acceptance of her as a person and a woman.

How did your father handle your transition to adulthood? To what extent has he given you the gift of his support and confidence? To what extent has he withheld these gifts? How has the separation from your father impacted your relationships with other men, including your husband?

As I write this chapter, my own daughter's transition to adulthood is still fresh in my mind. Several months ago I was privileged to walk her down the aisle to be united with a young man in marriage. Frankly, I wondered how I would handle my emotions that day. Her mother and I had weathered many storms as we watched Sheryl grow into adulthood and prepare to marry at age 27. We looked forward to her wedding day for many years. It was an intensely exciting day.

Some of my concern was over how I would handle conducting part of the wedding ceremony. But my fears were unfounded. I kept my composure and controlled my emotions (which is very important to men!). But two days later, as I sat and viewed the video of the wedding ceremony, something happened. As I watched Sheryl and I walk down the aisle together, my sense of loss mixed with joy burst to the surface and the tears came. And wouldn't you know it, right in the middle of my emotional outburst the phone rang! "Hi, Daddy," the familiar voice said. "What are you doing?" As I started to tell Sheryl what I was experiencing at the moment, my voice cracked and the words just wouldn't come out. Being sensitive and perceptive, Sheryl knew what I was experiencing. "Daddy," she responded warmly, "I'll always be your little girl." That didn't help settle my emotions at all! But I couldn't have asked for a better response. Yes, she's my adult, married daughter, but she's still my daughter. It's just a new relationship for us, part of a normal transitional stage in life.

Fathers do have an effect on their daughters. As you continue reading, keep these three important questions in mind:

1. In what way are you a product of your relationship with your father?
2. In what way would you like to change some of the results of your relationship with your father?
3. If you are the mother of a daughter, what is the pattern already developing between your husband and your daughter? Have you talked together about his relationship with her? Talk about it. Use the principles in this book to help you chart a positive course instead of just letting these relationships happen. Along with your husband, you as an adult daughter have an opportunity to positively influence your own daughter.

Notes

1. Linda S. Leonard, *The Wounded Woman* (Boston, MA: Shambhala Publications, Inc., 1983), adapted from p. 37.
2. Willard Gaylin, *Feelings* (NY: Harper and Row Publishers, Inc., 1979), pp. 22-23. Used by permission.
3. Suzanne Fields, *Like Father, Like Daughter* (Boston: Little, Brown and Co., 1983), p. 27.

4. Ibid., adapted from pp. 21-22.
5. George D. Goldman and Donald S. Milman, eds., *Modern Woman: Her Psychology and Sexuality* (Springfield, IL: Charles C. Thomas Publishers, 1969), pp. 181-182.
6. Leonard, *The Wounded Woman*, adapted from p. 17.
7. *Daddy's Little Girl*, William Woolfolk and Donna W. Cross. Reprinted by permission of the publisher, Prentice-Hall, Inc., Englewood Cliffs, New Jersey (1982), p. 35.
8. Gordon MacDonald, *The Effective Father* (Wheaton, IL: Tyndale House Publishers, 1977), adapted from pp. 226-227.
9. Leonard, *The Wounded Woman*, adapted from p. 9.
10. William S. Appleton, *Fathers and Daughters* (NY: Doubleday and Co., 1981), p. 41. Used by permission.
11. Nicky Marone, *How to Father a Successful Daughter* (NY: McGraw-Hill, 1988), p. 240.
12. Ibid., adapted from pp. 239-242.

THREE

Why Did Daddy Disappoint Me?

The crowded restaurant was humming with noisy lunch hour chatter. Two women huddled at a small table near mine, intently discussing their disappointments over the men they had been dating. They compared perplexing notes about how some of their dates treated them. After listening to her friend describe an experience of particular rudeness, Denise threw up her hands and blurted loudly, "Well, what did you expect? He's a man, isn't he?"

At Denise's sudden outburst, several patrons stopped talking and turned to stare at her. I enjoyed observing the different nonverbal responses of those who heard her. The men wore puzzled expressions or frowns, but the women either smiled knowingly or nodded their heads in agreement.

Denise's question is a good one: What do you expect from a man? I'd like to ask you a parallel question: What did you expect from your father? You had certain expectations as a child in your relationship with your dad, and you have expectations now as an adult daughter. Many of our expectations for people reflect our desires instead of our needs. Were your childhood expectations for your father realistic and attainable for him? Did your father fulfill all your childhood expectations? What about your present expectations? Are they being met by him? Conflicts occur when a father cannot or does not live up to his daughter's expectations for him, or when unfulfilled expectations become demands.

Fathers and daughters clash on expectations because men are different from women. Men are constructed differently inside and out. For example, a man's skin wrinkles later in life than a woman's skin—which many women consider unfair! And men talk about themselves less, but worry about themselves more, than women. Does that difference surprise you? Think about it: How many men open up and tell you what they are worried about?

Men possess different characteristics than women, and with these characteristics come limitations which often prevent fathers from fulfilling their daughters' expectations. Understanding male differences and limitations may help you understand why your father could not or would not live up to your ideals for him. This insight may also help you better understand your relationship with other men in your life: husband, close friends, fellow employees and sons.

The Weakness of Strength

Men like to be thought of as strong, stable and definitely in control. Some men appear to be programmed to tackle jobs, attack problems, surmount obstacles and overcome challenges aggressively and competitively. Many men thrive on achieving and winning, and some try to instill this tendency in their daughters.

Here is one description of a man that applies to many fathers:

> The armor plating he protects himself with is difficult to penetrate. He appears strong, stable, never rattled by emotions or feelings. He endeavors to dominate and outperform others but does not make it appear that much of an effort. He has relationships with other men built upon respect rather than close, intimate friendship. Intimate relationships are an enigma to him.[1]

A strong tendency to be strong and in control can be evident even in his relationship with household pets. Think about your father and his animals. Did he prefer dogs or cats? If he was like most men, dogs were his choice. Why? Men relish the loyalty and obedience of dogs. Dogs are devoted and submissive. When you call a dog he responds. But cats are basically independent and aloof unless they want food or attention. A man and a cat will often not get along because the man wants to be in control and a cat will not be controlled.

Was your father obsessed with his work? Many daughters have longed for the time and in-depth attention which a father funneled into his occupation or career. Since the primary arena for strength and competition in a man's life is his job, he tends to focus his attention, time and energy there rather than at home with the family. A man's success at work is a major contributor to his feelings of masculinity. His job affirms who he is and provides an outlet for his creative side. Unfortunately, men derive their sense of identity and self-esteem from their performance on the job. This high physical and emotional investment saps their attention and energy away from their families.

The inner masculine push to conquer and win has its down side. Nobody can win all the time, and strength doesn't always meet the needs of the women in his life. Here's one of the best descriptions I've read of a man's inner conflict:

> Men are raised to take charge,
>   but they cannot all be their own bosses.
> Men are raised to be primary providers,
>   but they find they are now living during
>   inflation and recession.
> Men are raised to focus on achievement,
>   but success is usually a momentary experience.
> Men are raised to stand on their own,
>   but they need support systems.
> Men are raised to express "strong" emotions,
>   but they often feel "weak" ones like fear and sad-
>   ness too.
> Men are raised to be team players,
>   but it's often "every man for himself."
> Men are raised to be Daddy's Big Boy,
>   but expected to remain Mommy's Little Man.
> Men are raised to be independent,
>   but urged to bond and nest.
> Men are raised to follow their dream,
>   but required to be realistic about security.[2]

The pressures which men exert on each other—and which society as a whole exerts on men—to perform, dominate, control and appear strong tends to make men brittle. They lack the flexibility of women. Men tend to override their own pain and weakness, which can cause them to lack sensitivity and empathy when responding to the pain and weakness of others. Women have greater ability to express strength or weakness, dependence or independence, passivity or dominance, emotionality or rationality, courage or fear without any of these traits threatening their self-esteem. But it is difficult for a man to move very far from the strong, in-control side of these characteristics. [3]

Do these descriptions apply in some ways to your father? If so, how did those tendencies affect your expectations of him? Did you expect warmth, tenderness and intimacy from him, only to be pushed aside by his drive for success and control? How did your father's penchant for strength color your view of other men in your life?

Even now your father may be blocking your expectations by his sometimes hard-headed masculine need for independence.

The Restrictions of Independence

Men tend to be independent and often prefer to have others lean on them rather than do any leaning themselves. Phrases like "I can do it myself," "I can figure it out myself" and "I can learn it myself" reflect their tendency not to ask for help.

Do you remember riding with your family in the car when your father was totally lost? Your mother would say, "There's a gas station, Dear. Let's stop and ask for directions." But your father replied, "I'm not lost. I can find the place myself." And he did find it, but it took him twice as long as it would have if he had stopped to ask directions.

Or you may have heard your mother offer a helpful suggestion to your father concerning a household project. In keeping with his masculine independence, he often discounted or ignored her idea. But the next day he came back with a "great new idea" he had come up with—which was really Mom's original suggestion in disguise!

Do you carry scars from your father's independence? As you grew older, did you expect him to value your ideas and suggestions, ask your advice in areas of your expertise, or seek your assistance with something he could no longer do? Even now your father may be blocking your expectations by his sometimes hard-headed masculine need for independence.

The Limitations of Emotional Control

What was your father like emotionally? Was he a feelings-oriented person or did he respond mainly with facts? How did he feel about himself, your mother and you, and how did he deal with his feelings? If he is still living, what feelings does he presently express in his interactions with you?

I have asked hundreds of women the following question over the last several years: "What emotions does your father express and how does he express them?" It's one of the questions you answered in chapter 1. The first response below reflects the typical picture of fathers and their emotions. Perhaps it is descriptive of your father. If not, you will probably see your father in one of the other responses gleaned from my research:

He only expresses anger in an open way. He does that by yelling and condemning.

I don't remember him really expressing much emotion. You can't really tell when he's excited about something and when he's frustrated. He just clams up.

Emotions and feelings? Oh, he expresses his disapproval very well, either stating it directly or just implying it. He can get pretty boisterous when he watches sports on TV. I really can't think of any positive emotion he expresses except his enthusiasm for his own hobbies.

Dad expresses anger. He does this through throwing temper tantrums and inflicting pain. He is addicted to pain and uses it to control others. The other feelings he shares are unhappiness, frustration and sadness, and he usually displays these continuously by complaining. Sometimes his feelings erupt in violent outbursts.

Other women were more fortunate in their relationships with their fathers since they were privileged to see a wider range of emotional responses. Many women reported that their fathers expressed compassion through crying and love through a special touch or hugs. Here are a few of their answers:

I have seen my father cry on numerous occasions, usually in a discussion about family differences. When he feels hurt, he tends to internalize it and blame himself.

Dad expresses most everything from sadness and crying to happiness and excitement. He really doesn't show much anger, but he can get tense.

My father expressed love verbally and through kind actions. When he was angry, he was honest and straightforward with his feelings. I've seen him grieve over the death of a family member. And I've seen him express joy verbally. This took awhile for him to learn, but he learned it from his kids and grand-kids.

Dad expressed joy through his face, sorrow through being reserved, frustrations by being brisk and busy, and love by showing and telling me.

Did you identify with any of the responses above? How did your father's emotional expression, or lack of it, affect you?

It's not surprising that men tend to be reluctant to express their feelings, since they also are reluctant to share other personal information about themselves. Many men don't feel the need for intimate sharing and closeness. This is unfortunate because it often isolates them from the women in their lives. If your father was quiet and inward, your mother probably felt isolated in their relationship, and perhaps you did as well.

Men are generally less responsive than women emotionally for several reasons. Some reasons are cultural and environmental. For example, men desire control, and since expressed feelings cannot be easily controlled, they are repressed. Many men are emotionally handicapped because they grew up without seeing emotions expressed positively by their male role models. Furthermore, most boys were not encouraged to learn an emotional/feeling vocabulary as they grew up. And many men consider the expression of feelings to be a feminine trait.

Another reason has to do with the way in which God created men and women to be respectively unique. Women use their brains holistically, whereas men shift from one side of the brain to the other. Women have a heightened sense of intuition because they have thousands more nerve connections between the left and right sides of the brain. About 75 percent of all men tend to be left-brain oriented, thinking analytically, sequentially and rationally. Some extreme left-brain men regard emotions and feelings as a foreign language! (For additional information on this subject, see *Understanding the Man in Your Life* [Word Books], by this author.)

Men sometimes go to great lengths to build walls which keep their emotions in and keep the feelings of others out. Some men end up becoming self-contained hermits. I like the way Ken Druck describes how men tend to appear emotionally unaffected and in control. Do any of these statements describe your father or the other men in your life?

Men rationalize a course of inaction by telling themselves, "What good is it going to do to talk about it? That's not going to change anything."

Men worry and worry internally, but never face what they really feel.

Men escape into new roles or hide behind old ones.

Men take the attitude that the "feelings" will pass and shrug them off as unimportant.

Men keep busy especially with work.

Men change one feeling into another—becoming angry instead of experiencing hurt or fear.

Men deny the feeling outright.

Men put feelings on hold—put them in the file drawer and tend to forget what they were classified under.

Feelings are confronted with drugs and alcohol.

Men are excellent surgeons. They create a "thinking bypass" to replace feelings with thought and logic.

Men sometimes avoid situations and people who elicit certain feelings in them.

Some men get sick or behave carelessly and hurt themselves so they have a reason to justify their feelings.[4]

The Silence of Shallow Communication

There is one other area of concern to consider when it comes to identifying the limitations of men and their impact on adult daughters: communication. Reflect on your relationship with your father. What was his communication style? Was his interaction with you extensive, or did you end up feeling unfulfilled when the two of you communicated? Were you on the same wave length, or did one of you share facts while the other shared feelings? Did your father tend to be an amplifier in conversations—giving sufficient details and using descriptive adjectives? Or was he a condenser—getting to the bottom line as quickly as possible? Did he stick to the point or amble around the barn a few times before you knew what he was talking about? Did he reveal personal information about himself and his feelings, or was he guarded? Did you feel that he understood you? Did he feel that you understood him? In your opinion, did you and your father communicate well?

In general, men are less adept at verbal communication than women. Men tend to talk about facts rather than emotions, wanting to exchange objective data rather than express subjective feelings. They are usually condensers instead of amplifiers, summarizing and getting to the point. Understanding these basic differences alone may give you insight into some of the difficulties in your relationship with your father. As a woman, you wanted to have an emotional exchange while your father was more interested in an information exchange. You wanted to "talk it out" while he wanted to "wrap it up." He probably failed to meet your expectations in communication.

Here's what a number of women between the ages of 20-35 said about their verbal interaction with their fathers. They were responding to the exercise you completed in chapter 1: "Describe how you and your father communicate(d)." The majority of the responses revealed the characteristic reticence of fathers to open up to their daughters in deep communication. Do some of the following responses reflect your relationship with your father?

> He was on one level and I was under him. We talked facts, no feelings or emotions.

> We don't communicate much.

> When I would try to talk with my father, I felt he did not always listen to my point of view. He seemed to have a hard time understanding my reasoning.

> I listen most of the time. I work hard at telling about myself because he usually doesn't ask probing ques-

tions. But we do well talking together. He does confide in me.

I wish we had better communication. We usually don't talk much about very personal things. But through the years I've always known I could talk with him at any time about anything.

Communication between my father and me were strained at best. Generally our conversations stayed at an impersonal "small talk" level.

Actually, I generally avoid him. When circumstances bring us together, we both treat each other quite carefully. We try not to get too close emotionally.

Even at this stage in our lives communication is forced and shallow. While growing up I *never* expressed how I truly felt. I obeyed his commands silently, but with an internal monologue of hostility running inside me. There was no physical interaction and eye contact was avoided. Our communication wasn't very pretty.

We see each other now about twice a year and the only communication that goes on between us is on the surface—our jobs, etc. I don't feel comfortable talking to him now about things that are really important to me, and he doesn't ask me any questions.

Other women enjoyed communication with their fathers which was more positive:

I felt I could always talk with my father without fear of rejection or insensitivity.

My father and I communicated by simply talking to each other. If we had any differences, we resolved them by compromising. If I chose not to talk, he would wait until I was ready to talk or he encouraged me to tell him how I felt. That was a real gift!

When I was younger he would always have the last word. Perhaps that happened because I would get too frustrated to keep talking. I would get nervous, tense and upset, and I'd lose my train of thought. It's much better now. We've both grown and I can share what I think and how I feel and he listens.

Usually we communicate rationally and peacefully. My father isn't so busy that I have to make an appointment with him. And he isn't unreachable. I can usually tell him whatever is on my mind, though my communication is closer with my mom.

What Makes Dad Tick?

There is one other factor to keep in mind as you strive to understand your father's characteristics and limitations. It's quite possible that you are unaware of some of the experiences your father had growing up which shaped his personality and behavior. Every man is different in a multitude of ways. Most of us fathers are not all that we could be. We haven't attained all that we were meant to be. Our weaknesses, failures and limitations create frustrations and inflict wounds in our daughters. Some wounded daughters choose to allow their poor relationship with their fathers to hinder them in their other relationships. Other women, however, choose to move ahead and not allow an imperfect father-daughter relationship to limit them or distort their perspective of the other men in their lives. It's a choice every daughter must make.

Some wounded daughters choose to allow their poor relationship with their fathers to hinder them in their other relationships.

Who is your father? I know that sounds like a strange question, but it really isn't. I've talked to many men and women who are acquainted with their fathers, but who have never dug deeply into their father's life and past to discover his personal history. Perhaps you are relatively uninformed about your father's life. If you made special effort to investigate his past history, you might understand better why he is the way he is and why your relationship has taken the shape it has.

The most direct way to get to know your father better is to ask him questions about his life. One method is to sit down with your father over your family photo album. As you leaf slowly through the pages, ask him about the people and places in the snapshots.

Another method is a planned personal interview using the list of questions presented here. Make an appointment with your father, and select a place where you won't be interrupted by the TV, phone, etc. Set aside at least an hour for the first meeting, aware that it may take more than one meeting to complete all the questions. Don't limit yourself to the questions listed here. Your father's responses may prompt other questions. Go ahead and ask them. You may want to use a tape recorder to capture all the details of his responses. The purpose of this meeting (you may also want to do this with your mother at another time) is to get to know your father as a unique individual.

If it is impossible to interview your father this way, or if he is deceased, you may want to use these questions to interview other relatives in order to fill in the gaps of your knowledge about him. I recently worked with a woman who learned a great deal about her deceased father by attending family reunions and talking with her father's brothers, sisters and childhood friends. It was a very enlightening and enjoyable experience for her.

Do you have mixed feelings about interviewing your father in this way? You may still be recovering from past wounds your father has inflicted. You may be afraid of the feelings which will surface during your discussion. You cannot predict what your father will say or how he will react. You cannot control your father's responses, but you can control your own. Perhaps reflecting on this passage from God's Word will prepare you for your discussion and help you keep everything in proper perspective:

> Therefore each of you must put off falsehood and speak truthfully to his neighbor, for we are all members of one body. "In your anger do not sin": Do not let the sun go down while you are still angry, and do not give the devil a foothold . . . . Do not let any unwholesome talk come out of your mouths, but only what is helpful for building others up according to their needs, that it may benefit those who listen. And do not grieve the Holy Spirit of God, with whom you were sealed for the day of redemption. Get rid of all

bitterness, rage and anger, brawling and slander, along with every form of malice. Be kind and compassionate to one another, forgiving each other, just as in Christ God forgave you (Eph. 4:25-27, 29-32).

FATHER INTERVIEW

What special memories do you have about your childhood?

How did you get along with each of your parents? What were they like?

What did you like and dislike about your parents?

What were your hurts and disappointments as a child?

What were your hobbies and favorite games?

How did you usually get into trouble?

How did you usually try to get out of trouble?

What did you enjoy about school and its activities?

What pets did you have? Which were your favorites and why?

What did you dream about doing when you were older?

Did you like yourself as a child? Why or why not?

Did you like yourself as a teenager? Why or why not?

What were your talents and special abilities?

What awards and special achievements did you win?

Did you have a nickname?

Who were your close friends? Where are they today?

What would you do on a hot summer afternoon?

Describe the area where you grew up—people, neighborhood, etc.

What were you afraid of? Do you have any of those fears today?

How did you get along with your brothers and/or sisters? If you had none, which relative were you closest to?

Who did you date and for how long? Where did you go on dates?

How did you feel when you liked someone and that person didn't care for you?

What was your spiritual life like as a child? As an adolescent?

How has being an adult changed your life?

How are you different today than you were 20 years ago? Ten years ago?

What have been your greatest disappointments? How have you handled them?

What have you learned from them that you would want me to learn?

If you could live your life over again, what would you do differently?

What do you want to be remembered for?

How did you meet my mother?

What was your first impression of her?

What was happening in your lives at the time you met?

How did your parents respond to your dating and engagement? How did her parents respond?

How did you make the decision to marry? Who proposed and how?

What have been the strengths and weaknesses of your marriage?

How did you get along with your in-laws at first?

How did you feel when my mother was expecting me?

What was it like to have children? How did it change your life?

What did you like and dislike about being parents?

What are your general impressions of me as a person?

What are your hopes and dreams for me?

What about me has brought you the greatest satisfaction? The greatest disappointment?

How have I changed as an adult?

How would you like me to grow and develop at this stage of my life?

In what way am I most like you? In what way am I least like you?

Notes

1. H. Norman Wright, *Understanding the Man in Your Life* (Waco, TX: Word Books, 1987), p. 16.
2. From THE MALE STRESS SYNDROME by Georgia Witkin-Lanoil, Ph.D. Copyright © 1986 by Georgia Watkin-Lanoil, Ph.D. Reprinted by permission of Newmarket Press, 18 East 48 Street, New York, NY 10017.
3. Herb Goldberg, *The New Male* (NY: Signet Books, 1979), adapted from p. 14.
4. Ken Druck with James C. Simmons, *The Secrets Men Keep* (NY: Doubleday and Co., 1985), adapted from pp. 35-36.

FOUR

Why Did Daddy Leave Me?

My father was not in the telephone book
in my city;
my father was not sleeping with my mother
in my home;
my father did not care if I studied the
piano;
my father did not care what I did;
and I thought my father was handsome and I loved
him
and I wondered
why
he left me alone so much,
so many years
in fact, but
my father
made me what I am
a lonely woman

without a purpose, just as I am
a lonely child
without any father. I walked with words, words, and
names, names. Father was not
one of my words.
Father was not
one of my names.[1]

As a father, I often traveled away from home for two
or three days at a time while my daughter Sheryl was
growing up. Every night I was away, I called home to talk
to my wife Joyce and to Sheryl. I knew what I would hear
from Sheryl every time she picked up the phone: "Daddy,
when are you coming home?" I also knew what I would
hear when I arrived home. She would come running to
meet me at the front door excitedly screaming, "Daddy's
home!" She had been waiting for me, expecting me to
return.

Many daughters have waited in vain for their fathers to
return, because some fathers leave and never return.
Fathers leave their families for many reasons. Some just
desert their wives and children irresponsibly and disap-
pear. Others divorce their wives, but continue to visit
their children occasionally. Still others are taken from their
families by an early death. And some fathers remain in the
home physically, but desert their families emotionally.

In Tennessee Williams's play, "The Glass Menagerie,"
Laura's father abandoned his family years earlier, never to
be heard from again. Laura's brother, who is the narrator
in the play, points to the prominently displayed, larger-
than-life portrait of their gallantly smiling father. His comment reveals the enormous unconscious influence the
departed father still exerts on his children:

This is our father who left us long ago. He was a telephone man who fell in love with long distances; he gave up his job with the telephone company and skipped the light fantastic out of this town . . . . The last we heard of him was a picture postcard from Mazatlan, on the Pacific coast of Mexico, containing a message of two words: "Hello—Good-bye!" and no address.[2]

The Daughter Who Is Left Behind

What happens to a daughter when a father leaves either through physical or emotional abandonment, divorce or death? Perhaps your father left you for some reason during your childhood or adolescence. You may have women friends who were left behind by their fathers. Have you sorted through your feelings about that loss? Have your friends described their feelings to you?

Here's what one woman said whose father died when she was three:

Most women have a man that got away, a man that they have loved and lost. For us, that man was father, the first man that we had ever loved. With his presence, he had introduced us to the delight of being the female recipient of male love. With his disappearance, he had taught us the precariousness of love. Whether he died or abandoned us, we felt rejected.[3]

For many women, father's leaving was a betrayal. It contained the seeds of the feelings of abandonment. And since father wasn't present, the surviving daughter often idealized him, magnifying his strengths and forgetting his weaknesses. Her idealized father became the standard against which all other men in her life were measured. Father was gone, but his "presence" still affected her life.

When a father exits a daughter's life for some reason, he vacates one of the most significant roles he should play in her life: the development of her autonomy and independence.

A young teacher described what happened to her when her father left home through a divorce:

"I always felt it was important to stay close to my father. He was an outgoing, cheerful man. I never could understand what he saw in my mother. When they separated I was nine years old. I had absolutely no doubt that she was at fault. If I could have, I would have chosen to live with my father. But he traveled so much—he was a regional sales manager for a liquor company—that I couldn't live with him even if Mother had been willing to let me.

"Mother tried to turn me and my younger sister against him. I never let her get away with that. He sent money to support us and that meant he loved us. When Mother spoke against him I wouldn't listen. I would tell my sister how Mother lied.

"When Father came and took us away for a day or maybe for a weekend I felt it was Christmas. I dreamed of growing older and being able to look after him. I would keep house for him and cook and never make the mistakes Mother made that drove him away."

Often it takes years for a daughter to come to a realistic assessment of her absent father.[4]

When a father exits a daughter's life for some reason, he vacates one of the most significant roles he should play in her life: the development of her autonomy and independence. In his own way, a father helps his daughter relinquish her attachment to her mother. A young woman wants to be independent, but she is somewhat hesitant, tentative and insecure about leaving mother's apron strings. Her father, the strongest influence in her life outside her mother, encourages her independence by affirming her importance as an individual. He "courts" her toward autonomy through his attention to her, his interest in her and his verbal encouragement of her strengths and uniqueness.

That's the ideal, the way it should be, the way it is for many daughters. But for many others whose fathers have departed, that vital role goes unplayed. Do you identify with the ideal—a father at home who lovingly encouraged you to find your place in the world? Or was the development of your identity and independence stunted because your father left the family during your childhood or adolescence?

When a Father Dies

What is it like for a little girl to know her father for awhile only to have him snatched away from her by death? Who can really understand the impact that a father's death has on a child? If the death was tragic or totally unexpected,

the grief may seem insurmountable. If death was a lingering process, it is equally difficult for a child to comprehend
and accept. Grief, the mental distress we suffer over a
loss, is the most agonizing, painful and draining emotion
and activity a human can experience. It is frightening in its
intensity for us as adults. What must it be like for a young
child to experience something so traumatic which is
beyond her understanding and control?

A child between the ages of three and six is at a stage
in life called the magic years. When a girl's father dies during this stage, she may play games and answer questions
about death which indicate that she sees it as reversible.
She may say something like, "Let's take Daddy to the hospital again to make him alive" or "Daddy needs some rest
and then he will wake up." One four-year-old, whose
father drove a red Camaro before he died, ran after every
red Camaro she saw driving by yelling, "Daddy! Daddy!"

A daughter at this age may believe that her own misbehavior or negative thoughts about her father caused his
death. One woman told me, "For years I actually believed
that I caused my father's death because I was mad at him.
That false belief took its toll on my life over the years."

If the daughter is older—between six and 11—when
her father dies, she may ask numerous detailed questions
about his death in her attempt to overcome the loss. A
child must be encouraged to deal with the emotional
impact of her father's leaving or she will continue in the
confusion depicted in this poem:

> And you asked where he went
> And they said:
> Heaven.
> And they took you to a field of tombstones and
> columbine

They said:
This is where his perfect body lay.
And you were confused
now there were two of him
and none for you.[5]

Pat, a 30-year-old mother, sat in my office sharing her story of losing her father when she was two and a half. I asked her what she remembered about the experience.

"I really didn't understand death at the time," she replied. "But I did react to my father leaving me. From what my mother said, I started acting like a brat. I kept asking where my father was, and my aunt kept responding, 'He's gone away on a long trip.' So I thought he was coming home again.

"Fortunately, my mother overheard her one day and said, 'No, Daddy is not on a long trip. Daddy died.' Then she told me about death. She also helped me express all my feelings during the next months—even years. I didn't bottle up my feelings. I really appreciate my mother's help in letting me grieve."

Pat was indeed fortunate. She was able to work through her loss. In their attempt to protect their grieving children, some mothers mask not only their own feelings, but their children's feelings as well by shading the truth about a father's death. Their attempts at protection, however, usually fail. In her book, *A Child's Parent Dies*, Erna Furman says, "Children are so observant of and sensitive to their parents' moods and nuances of behavior that, in our experience, it is impossible to spare them from knowing or to deceive them about the true nature of events."[6]

It may be heartbreaking for a mother to see the anguish of her daughter, but not being truthful about her father's death is even more devastating. Children are quick to perceive if a parent is hiding something. A mother's attempt to withhold the truth will magnify her daughter's feelings of rejection and abandonment at this time. She already feels left behind by her father; now she feels left out by her mother—totally abandoned!

Sometimes children don't feel anything when a father dies. This is often the case when the father was a strong and stable factor in the home, but failed to supply the necessary physical and emotional contact for his daughter. This daughter is emotionally deprived. Early on she learns to avoid the fear of abandonment and isolation by denying feelings and pain. Having trained herself this way, she feels little or nothing when her father abandons her through death.

The death of a parent, especially a father, is traumatic. But it's even more traumatic when the surviving parent fails to respond to the children with empathy or does not openly discuss with them their mutual loss. Repressed mourning in childhood is a negative factor which continues to affect the individual into adulthood.

Are you harboring uncompleted grief or repressed mourning from the death of your father (or another close relative) during your childhood or adolescence? Do you know someone else who may not have dealt adequately with her feelings about a close personal loss? You may be suffering consequences from that repression which you don't need to suffer.

What are the results of repressed mourning? Renee's experience reflects what many women suffer when they fail to deal with their feelings at the time of a father's death. Renee's father died when she was seven, and she was raised from then on in a fatherless home.

"Here I am, 47 years old," she began. "I feel as though I have been sad all my life. Suffering has been my middle name. Mother told us to be strong and move ahead. So every time I started to cry, I would try to stifle it. But I felt as though I was short-circuiting something which needed to happen."

"Perhaps you've wanted to cry for your father all these years and nobody would let you," I replied. "You've been carrying around inside you this container of tears and sadness and nobody has invited you to open the floodgates and let it all pour out." Renee looked surprised at first, then she nodded in agreement. "It's all right for you to grieve now," I continued. "It's not too late. Why not let your sadness and tears flow." And she did.

When a woman is unable to fulfil her grieving and mourning in childhood, she may be haunted for years—as Renee was—with an unexplained sadness which she cannot understand. There are some extreme cases where repressed mourning in a daughter has led to an inability to love another person such as her husband. Since she still carries unresolved grief from her previous loss, she is fearful that anyone else she opens her heart to may also be ripped out of her life.

Repressed mourning over any loss will affect your life. It's important for you to understand this about your past and to keep it in mind for the future concerning other loved ones you will eventually lose through death. Grieving is normal. It is God's way of helping us move forward in life. Scripture describes many characters who experienced tragic losses and grieved over them.

But if the expression of grief is repressed in some way, you may experience unexplained sadness, an inability to express love or emotional commitment, or a total denial of any feelings. However, an early acceptance of your loss will aid in the process of going on with your life. Robert Veninga says, "Once you have experienced the seriousness of your loss, you will be able to experience the wonder of being alive."[7]

I Never Knew My Father

Some women were infants when their fathers died. They never had the opportunity to know their fathers. They have no personal memories to draw upon. All they have is photographs, home movies and what their mothers and other relatives tell them. As a result, the father's critical, unique role in developing his daughter's physical and sexual self-image went unfulfilled. Also, the lack of a father's affection, both verbal and physical, creates in her either a deep longing for intimacy or a reactionary fear of close contact.

Nadine, a woman whose father was killed during World War II three months before she was born, talked about never knowing her father: "No father ever existed in my experience. The words Dad, Daddy and Father were foreign words for me. I've never called anybody by those names. I can refer to 'my father,' but the words are stilted and seem quite awkward to me.

"I guess I have a romanticized view of my father. I never experienced a father who was disappointed or disillusioned, or who struggled against middle age. I never saw him upset by his parents or quarreling with my mother. Yes, I've idealized him and learned to live without him. When I was younger I believed that not having a father had no affect on me. But I was wrong. It was later in life that I realized the vacuum that existed within me."

Nadine went on to describe the effect being fatherless had on her as she was growing up: "Mom finally remarried when I was nine, but her new husband and I never clicked. It seems like I went through high school and college in a destructive way. I think I wanted men to cater to me. I could never get enough attention. I was greedy. I wanted everything for myself. And often I didn't care what happened to others or myself. I just wanted others to care for me. I'm not a psychologist, but it seems that I wanted from everyone else what I never received from my father."

Nadine may not have been a psychologist, but her diagnosis of the problem wasn't far off. Many women who never knew their fathers respond to the world in a greedy, grasping, destructive and conscienceless manner. They want the world around them to supply them with what they missed.[8]

The Impact of Fatherlessness

Why does a father's absence have such a great impact on a daughter when the mother is still present? Ironically, when a father dies, it is quite common for the mother to leave the daughter also. She leaves physically in the sense that she may need to go back to work, spending many hours a day away from her daughter. She may also leave emotionally. As a single parent, she is stressed out from the time and energy she spends working and keeping up the home, denying her daughter sufficient emotional contact.

Sometimes the impact of a departing father has the opposite effect on a mother-daughter relationship. Instead of neglecting her daughter emotionally, a widowed mother may actually turn to her child for the support, comfort and nurturing she once received from her husband. Some mothers become overly involved with their daughters. And since father is not there to help his daughter move away from her mother and become independent, some daughters become overly dependent on their mothers.

Father's absence also follows his daughter into the very important area of her involvement with men. Some widowed mothers may become overly cautious with their daughters' involvement with men. Others react differently, encouraging involvement because they believe that daughters without fathers need husbands to take care of them.

No man can compete with a woman's idealized image of her departed father. Every man is an inadequate substitute for her fantasy.

As a fatherless young woman begins looking for a man to share her life with, she may carry with her an idealized image of her father. She measures each prospective mate against this perfect image, always looking for the nonexistant perfect man. But this process leads to major disappointments. No man can compete with a woman's idealized image of her departed father. Every man is an inadequate substitute for her fantasy. As a result, fatherless women are much more likely to shy away from intimacy. They're not about to give much of themselves to "second rate" men. Thus, their relationships with men are usually shallow.

Many fatherless women pour their energies into work as a substitute for the fathering they never had. It's true that many women become successful in careers *because* of the encouragement of their fathers. But it is also true that many other women succeed *without* a father's encouragement. Their work may be a solution to their childhood sorrow. Or it may be a reaction against the dependency they saw in their mothers and wish to avoid. Achievement can become a substitute for loss without the risk of intimacy and commitment.

Consider some of the well-known women who either lost their fathers in childhood or grew up not knowing their fathers. Helen Gurley Brown, editor-in-chief of *Cosmopolitan*, lost her father in adolescence. Perhaps the lack of a father's appreciation contributed to her driving need to learn how to calculate charm. Her magazine is devoted to helping women find, entice and keep men.

Isak Dinesen, a Danish writer who was twice nominated for a Nobel prize, lost her father at the age of nine. Eleanor Roosevelt lost her father just before her tenth birthday. She had promised her father that she would grow up to be a woman he could be proud of. After her father's death, Eleanor dedicated herself to continue the causes her father believed in. She did what many fatherless women have done: She validated and extended her father's existence through her own. This was true of Bess Truman and Rosalynn Carter, who lost their fathers through death, and Jacqueline Kennedy and Nancy Reagan, who lost their fathers through divorce.

Barbra Streisand is an interesting example of a woman who sought to recreate in her work the longed-for image of her father. Remember the film *Yentl?* Streisand devoted years of her life to that film, including directing it. She said *Yentl* gave her the chance to "make" a father. In the film she made him warm and kind, wise and compassionate. She made him the kind of father every woman would like to have. Perhaps she chose this story because it involves the death of the female character's father. The woman then keeps him "alive" by carrying on the love and reverence for books and learning he had passed on to her.

Many have criticized Barbra Streisand for her seemingly unnatural drive and ambition. But, as with many other women, her ambition is her way of filling the void created by a father who left no image in her life.

We have discussed the effects in a daughter's life of losing a father through death. In the next chapter we will look at father loss through divorce and its far-reaching effects on the daughter he leaves behind.

Notes

1. Diane Wakoski, as quoted in *The Wounded Woman* by Linda S. Leonard, Ohio University Press, 1982. Reprinted with the permission of Ohio University Press, Athens, Ohio.
2. Tennessee Williams, *The Glass Menagerie* (NY: New Directions, 1970), p. 23.
3. Elyce Wakerman, *Father Loss* (Garden City, NY: Doubleday and Co., 1984), p. 13.
4. *Daddy's Little Girl: The Unspoken Bargain Between Fathers and Their Daughters* by William Woolfolk and Donna Woolfolk Cross © 1982. Reprinted by permission of the publisher, Prentice-Hall, Inc., Englewood Cliffs, NJ.
5. Wakerman, *Father Loss*, p. 41.
6. Erna Furman, *A Child's Parent Dies* (New Haven, CN: Yale University Press, 1974), p. 18.
7. Robert Veninga, *A Gift of Hope* (Boston: Little, Brown and Co., 1985), p. 71.
8. Martha Wolfenstein, adapted from a panel discussion, "Effects on Adults of Object Loss in the First Five Years." Annual meeting of the American Psychoanalytic Association, Los Angeles, May 1975. *Scientific Proceedings* (1975), p. 660.

FIVE

Why Doesn't Daddy Live Here Anymore?

Several months ago I attended a wedding and was quite surprised at what I saw. I'm sure it happens more frequently than I am aware of, but it still caught me off guard. The bride was escorted down the aisle to meet the groom not by one father, but two! Her stepfather was on one side and her natural father was on the other. Both fathers kissed the bride, then sat down on either side of the girl's mother. I wondered what the bride was thinking and feeling as she clutched the arms of both fathers. Her natural father left the home when she was quite young. She had contact with him over the years, but was raised by her stepfather. Her story is the story of millions of children in our country whose natural fathers have left home.

Here's another story about a daughter whose father deserted her through divorce:

"Come into the living room, children. We have something we need to tell you." That's how our parents told us they were not going to be together anymore. After they told us they were divorcing, I sat under the table and my mind replayed again and again the words my father said. I didn't know then what it all meant, but I soon learned.

After Dad left, I looked through the drawers where he kept his clothes and found an old sweat shirt he left behind. I hid it in my room and kept it for years. I would cling to it when I was lonely for him.

My father came back to see us a few times, but his visits became less and less frequent. Finally his visits stopped completely. I always wondered where he went. I wondered if he thought about us very much. I hoped that he did. But I guess I'll never know.

What happens when a father leaves the home, and how does his departure affect his daughter? Did you experience abandonment by your father through a divorce in the home? How did it impact your life? I'm sure many of your friends or acquaintances are victims of divorce. How were their lives impacted?

When a father dies there is a sense of closure to the relationship and an opportunity to say a final good-bye. A daughter goes through a period of mourning which is rather predictable. But where is the mourning period after a divorce? A child left behind by a deserting father feels uncertain. "Is Father coming back or not?" she wonders. The child doesn't know whether the loss will be permanent or temporary. The occasional birthday card, the weekly phone call and the weekend visits and vacations keep alive the fantasy that father might return.

The Disruption of Divorce

A couple may resolve their problems through divorce, but the problems caused by the divorce are just beginning for the children. Often a child fears that she may have brought about the divorce, causing her painful guilt. Some daughters, without the love and affirmation of their fathers, look to their mothers for extra amounts of attention, which the physically and emotionally stressed divorcee may not be able to supply. A daughter needs the guidance of adults to understand the process of divorce and work through the adjustment.

Judith Wallerstein, a psychologist who has worked with more than 2,000 families in various stages of separation, divorce and remarriage, conducted a ten-year study of 60 divorced California families. The study is reported in her book, *Second Chances: Men, Women and Children a Decade after Divorce*. Ms. Wallerstein followed up on these 60 families at five and ten year intervals. She discovered that only ten percent of the couples enjoyed happier and fuller lives after their divorces. Two-thirds of the children had poor relationships with their fathers, which included fathers who were completely estranged from the family as well as those who visited their children regularly. Seventy-five percent of the children felt rejected by their fathers.

Many family specialists feel that divorce may have a "sleeper effect" on daughters. The effect may not be evident until adolescence and young adulthood. Many daughters seem to feel derailed by divorce and anxious as they move into adolescence and adulthood. They are afraid of being betrayed by men and attribute this fear to their parents' divorce.[1]

Janet is a classic example of what can occur when parents divorce and the father leaves home. At the age of 14, several years after her parents' divorce, Janet began experiencing depression and losing weight. She didn't appear to have any desire to come out of her depression.

In time it became evident that she was filled with rage over "what her father had done." But, as with many young girls, Janet wouldn't admit her anger. When her mother tried to discuss the situation, Janet tended to support her father and told her mother not to speak negatively about him. But this only increased Janet's internal conflict since she was aware of how the divorce and her depression were affecting her mother, and Janet felt sorry for her.

Janet also struggled with guilt, feeling responsible for the divorce. Two years prior to her father's departure, Janet, a typical adolescent, became more verbal, defiant and unresponsive at home. When her father left, she was afraid that it was her behavior which had pushed him away from the home. Janet loved her father and her mother, but loving one tended to make her feel disloyal to the other. Her inner life was a multitude of conflicts.

When there is a family breakup, the daughter often develops and believes a number of myths. In Janet's case, the myths sounded something like this:

My mother was a good person and my father victimized her unfairly.

My father left because he couldn't handle my rebellious attitude. He probably also blamed Mom for the way I was.

My father left us because he was self-centered, caring only for what he wanted and not what we needed.

My mother was hurt so much through this that she can't make it without my taking care of her.

If I recover and am happy again, that will hurt mother. She won't be able to handle it.

I have to pick one parent over the other. I can't be loving and loyal to both of them. If I show love to Dad and spend time with him, Mother will be upset.

I can't show Dad how angry I am since he is treating me nicely right now. I don't want to push him away since he might never come back.

My father's new girlfriend is responsible for his leaving. But I can't be angry with her either.[2]

If a daughter is to survive abandonment by her father, these myths must be exploded and replaced by the truth. Sadly, often the other adults in the daughter's life—including her mother—are unable to move her successfully through this process.

Feelings of the Fatherless Daughter

A daughter who was abandoned by her father carries numerous feelings into adulthood. She may doubt her self-worth, suspicious that she failed her role in keeping the family together. She wonders what she did, or did not do, which caused the family to break up. Jean said to me in a counseling session one day, "I know of a number of families where the parents didn't care for each other. But they stayed together so it wouldn't damage their kids. For those fathers, the kids were worth sticking around. But I guess I wasn't worth even that. How do you think that makes me feel about myself?"

She may carry unresolved anger over being left by her father, which taints her relationship with other men. She wants a man in her life, but she is unsure about trusting him. Any violation of trust from the men she cares about is further proof to her that she can't trust any man. She wants to be loved and she wants to be lovable. But anger, mistrust and fear of intimacy with men can keep her from giving herself to a man.

When an adult daughter of a divorced father approaches marriage, she may have mixed feelings about his involvement in her ceremony. Occasionally I am asked by a woman in premarital counseling how her father should participate. He abandoned her at a young age, but now wants to be involved in her life again. He even wants to walk her down the aisle. "I would much rather have my stepfather walk me down the aisle," most women tell me. "I feel closer to him than to my dad. In fact, I resent the fact that my father wants to walk back into my life now. I didn't leave him; he left me. I have no feelings for him as a father. My stepfather gave me what my father withheld from me."

When a father leaves home through divorce, the relationship between the surviving mother and daughter is significantly affected.

Strong, negative feelings often follow an abandoned daughter into her marriage. June is a prime example. She came to me for counseling with her husband Jim. Jim couldn't understand why his behavior bothered June so much. Whenever she tried to express her concerns to him, Jim would either turn on the TV, bury his face in the newspaper or leave the room. Jim felt that he had heard what she had to say, so why continue the discussion? But his behavior said more to her. She felt abandoned by Jim, and it wasn't until she explained her childhood relationship with her father during our session that Jim finally understood:

> When I was four months old, my father left my mother, and I never knew him. She married my stepfather three years later and he left us when I was six. Three years later she married my second stepfather and he stayed for another three years. By the time I was 12 years old, I had been abandoned by the three most important men in my life. Even my mother left me during those years by shutting me out of her life.
>
> I married you, Jim, hoping that a man would never abandon me again. When you walk out when I'm trying to talk to you, or turn on the TV or pick up the paper, a flood of terrible feelings from the past surges up inside of me. I try to talk in such a way that you'll stay and listen, but sometimes I don't succeed. I guess I'm tired of trying to make everything right, just like I tried to do as a child. I couldn't make the men stay then, and now I'm afraid that I can't keep you either.

Does June's situation sound familiar to you? Did you grow up feeling that you had to make everything "right" in order to please your father?

Fatherless Daughters and Their Mothers

When a father leaves home through divorce, the relationship between the surviving mother and daughter is significantly affected. A major study on this topic indicated that fatherless daughters actually spend less time alone with their mothers than other girls.[3] The daughters studied felt they received less affection from their mothers after the separation, and that too much was expected of them. They understood that their mothers didn't have sufficient time for them because of work. But many of them felt emotionally trapped in the situation. They were angry at their fathers for abandoning them, but he wasn't available to be the target of their anger. So a daughter often felt like venting her anger on her mother, blaming her for the father's absence. At the same time, the girl felt the need to squelch her anger because Mom was all she had left, and she needed her more than ever. The pattern of daughters of divorce repressing their emotions is prevalent.

Often a mother places more responsibility on her daughter after a divorce. And some daughters take on more adult responsibilities as a means of surviving their loss. If a daughter is the eldest child or an only child, she often pushes herself to assume a much more responsible role in the home. She feels the need to become an adult, filling the void created by the missing father.

One writer shared an interesting perspective on this "pseudo-maturity": "The early adoption of adult behavior thus serves two very definite functions for her. By being good and helpful, she ensures mother's continued acceptance and presence. And by being strong, she tries to resist identification with someone whose low self-esteem is threatening to her own."[4] Often a woman who loses her husband experiences diminishing self-esteem, appearing weak when her daughter needs to see her as strong. The daughter does not want to appear weak like her mother, so she learns the value of controlling her emotions like an adult.

When her father exits, a young daughter may also feel constrained to fill the role of adult companion for her mother as well as remaining a daughter. The girl functions as her mother's peer as well as her child. But in so doing she develops adult independence ahead of schedule and builds a defensive structure against childlike intimacy. This artificial maturity arrives much too early.[5] The girl must learn to develop and operate within a different relationship with her mother.

During a counseling session, one of my clients summarized the experiences of thousands of women when she described herself, and her relationship with her mother, in a fatherless home:

> Norm, the reason I'm here is I'm a survivor. I had to be. I know I am insecure emotionally, but I do survive. With no father since I was six, I learned to grow up fast. Perhaps I'm stronger today because of what I went through. Mom worked to keep us alive. She was tired at night and couldn't listen to all my trivia, so I learned to handle my problems myself.
>
> I worked at odd jobs at age 12 and discovered I had something to offer. By 17 I had saved enough for a car, even before I graduated from high school.
>
> I have a good job now and know I'll make it financially. But when it comes to men, that's where I'm insecure. And you know what? I would much rather have a man in my life than a career. My job was more of a necessity to survive; it was not my first choice.

The Deserted Teenage Girl

What happens when a fatherless daughter approaches her adolescent years? Are there differences between these girls and others who come from two-parent homes?

Although many exceptions and variations may appear, some significant trends suggest that differences do exist.

Researcher Dr. Pollard says:

> Teenage daughters involved in a divorce situation feel sad and confused. They blame themselves, at least in part, for what happened. Initially, their fathers are romanticized as they wish to remember them rather than as they were. As the daughter grows older, her still-present visible mother also changes. She doesn't grow in intelligence or stature or authority—not in the daughter's opinion. She gets older, more nervous, more interfering and bothersome. Only father remains beyond change—the daddy of memory.[6]

Often fatherless daughters are more awkward or ill at ease as they approach the teen years. They lack not only the interaction with their fathers, but also an ongoing model of the father-mother relationship, a necessary reflection of male-female interaction.

E. Mavis Hetherington discovered that fatherless girls interacted with males differently than girls from two-parent homes:

> Adolescent girls who had grown up without fathers repeatedly displayed inappropriate patterns of behavior in relating to males. Girls whose fathers had died exhibited severe sexual anxiety, shyness, and discomfort around males. Girls whose fathers were absent because of divorce exhibited tension and inappropriately assertive, seductive, or sometimes promiscuous behavior with male peers and adults . . . . Girls whose fathers had died spoke significantly less

with a male interviewer and were generally more silent than any other group of subjects. Girls whose parents were divorced tended to talk more with a male interviewer than with a female interviewer. [7]

The daughter of divorce often uses the divorce to justify her distrust of men, so the young men in her life are at a disadvantage in the dating experience. She reasons that if her father is lacking, all other men must be lacking as well. Daughters whose fathers died tend to perceive husbands and fathers as having predominantly positive characteristics. But daughters who came from divorced homes tend to perceive most men as having negative characteristics. [8]

Many fatherless daughters rush into marriage . . . looking to their husbands to rescue them from past disappointments and heartache at the hands of their fathers.

When adolescent daughters approach marriageable age, they are apt to respond to marriage prospects in one of two contrasting ways. Many fatherless daughters rush into marriage with unrealistic optimism and expectations. Often they are looking to their husbands to rescue them from past disappointments and heartache at the hands of their fathers. These fantasy-like hopes are seldom realized.

Other daughters resist marrying because of the fear of intimacy. They balk at opening themselves to men because they are afraid they will eventually drive their husbands away like they suspect they drove their fathers away. Others fear that their utopian visions for married life will disintegrate because that's what happened to their parents' marriages.

Yes, there are some negative consequences and long-term effects from being left behind by a divorcing or deserting father. Many women feel rejected by their fathers, and many were indeed rejected. Often they do not feel they can trust their emotional responses. They learned to value repression and they matured too soon. Daughters who may be affected the most are those who never knew their fathers and those whose fathers were outwardly indifferent before they abandoned their families.

But the redeeming factor which helps many women through the ordeal of fatherlessness is a sensitive mother, one who works hard to defeat the negative effects of no father in the home. If her mother manifests positive and balanced coping skills, the daughter is able to learn from this modeling. These positive coping skills counter the negative effects of repression, rejection and premature maturity. The availability of outside support systems make a difference in daughters' lives as well. Many mothers who don't remarry immediately or at all find significant mature men who can provide some of the positive masculine modeling that their daughters lost.

But not every abandoned daughter is fortunate enough to have such a positive response to her loss. What about those who are still affected? What about you? What about your friends? Is there hope for recovery after father loss? Yes, there is![9]

Notes

1. Joan Libman, "No 'Happily Ever After' in Divorce," *Los Angeles Times* (January 30, 1989), Part IV, adapted from p. 8.
2. Howard Halpern, *Cutting Loose*, (NY: Bantam Books, 1977) adapted from p. 178.
3. Elyce Wakerman, *Father Loss* (Garden City, NY: Doubleday and Co., 1984), adapted from p. 13.
4. Ibid., p. 131.
5. Ibid., adapted from pp. 126-134.
6. *Daddy's Little Girl: The Unspoken Bargain Between Fathers and Their Daughters* by William Woolfolk with Donna Woolfolk Cross © 1982. Reprinted by permission of the publisher, Prentice-Hall, Inc., Englewood Cliffs, NJ.
7. E. Mavis Hetherington, "Girls Without Fathers," *Psychology Today*, (February 1973), pp. 44-52.
8. Ibid., adapted from pp. 44-52.
9. Wakerman, *Father Loss*, adapted from chapters 2, 3, 6, 9, 10 and 12.

SIX

Who Was That Phantom?

"My father is there, but he's not there—do you know what I mean? He's around the house, but he's not really a part of us. His body takes up space, but he's not involved. If a person is there, you expect him to be involved in your life in some way, don't you? My father isn't. He's distant. Some of my girlfriends with divorced parents have fathers who are more interested and involved in their lives than mine is. I feel left out—cheated. It isn't fair."

Margaret's anger toward her father had been brewing inside her for years. As she told me her story, she finally faced her feelings about him. Her comments reflect the frustration of many women whose fathers are not dead, divorced or physically separated from the family, but who are socially and emotionally estranged from the family. As another woman I counseled said about her father, "Sometimes I ask myself, 'Who is that stranger?'"

I call these men phantom fathers. Some phantom fathers spend sufficient time in the home, but their interaction with their daughters is very superficial. This man may talk a little with his daughter about the news, work and sports, but he never reveals very much of himself. Some phantoms are little more than walking checkbooks for their families. They pay for everything, but they are emotionally detached from everyone.

Jeanine, another of my counselees, described her phantom father this way: "My dad took time to take me places, but usually it was with his friend and his daughter. I liked being with the other girl; we had good times together. But our dads usually gave us money to go entertain ourselves while the two of them talked, ate or did things they enjoyed. Everyone kept saying what a great father he was because he spent time with me. But Dad never really got to know me. I feel sad now about being left out. If people only knew what Dad was really like!"

Some phantom fathers, like Jeanine's dad, appear to be "nice guys." They are easygoing, agreeable and likeable. They are consistent, stable and passive, but they don't express any of their feelings to their family members. This dad is very cautious since he doesn't really trust his own feelings or the responses of others to his feelings. He often fails his family by tending to store up his hurts and complaints, expressing them in passive-aggressive behaviors such as silence, forgetfulness or tardiness. A daughter will have difficulty developing any closeness or emotional intimacy with such a father.

Standing on the Sidelines

The classic phantom father is rarely seen. He is a devoted provider who believes that the best way to demonstrate love to his family is to give them a good life. He works ten to 15 hours a day, six days a week, leaving little time for him to be with his family or to get close to them emotionally. Achievement is everything to him. His interaction with family members lacks substance.

This father is often called a bystander. He is a father in word, but not often in deed. He might be in physical proximity to his daughter, but he isn't close to her. There is a physical presence, but not an emotional nearness. Some daughters feel like they are invisible to their phantom fathers. Because Dad is unaware of his daughter's inner struggles and desire for closeness, his daughter ends up feeling like an ignored shadow.

The bystanding father seems to his daughter to be a man with secrets, and she may exert tremendous energy trying to discover these secrets: "Is he disappointed in me? Is he fearful and full of anxiety, incapable of relating to the real world? Is he filled with such anger against the world that it is now being redirected toward me?" These secrets can become an unspoken burden upon a daughter.

The daughter who tries in vain to get involved with a bystanding father often ends up feeling misplaced. Sometimes she even feels responsible for his apathy. Donna put it so well during a counseling session: "What's wrong with me? What bad things did I do which caused my father to be so distant?" Fortunately, Donna came to realize that the defect was not in her and that she was not responsible for his behavior.

The bystanding phantom father is a disappointment in many ways. He is a poor model for work because he places his job, overtime and advancement ahead of his family. He is a poor model for love because he is emotionally closed, distant and secretive toward those he says he loves. As his daughter's first example of a man, this father distorts her concept of how a man should behave, causing her to believe that all men are distant and detached like her father. Unfortunately, this early disappointment with a withdrawn bystanding father provokes some women to turn away from men and seek the company of women for companionship and love.[1]

Some fathers are bystanders in their daughters' lives because they are physically absent due to work. Susan had such an absentee father. One day she shared her experience with me:

> My father traveled as a sales representative. Whenever he left, I was disappointed. It was boring around the house without him because my mother wasn't much fun. When I knew he was coming home, I would get so excited because he would always bring me a gift. I couldn't do my homework or anything. I would even wait for him near the window, listening for his car. When I was real young I would fall asleep waiting.
>
> When he returned home I would share with him everything I had learned in school and tell him about all my activities. He talked with me, hugged me and played with me for a couple of days. But then I felt let down again because he worked such long hours at the office. He didn't have time to do with me what my friend's dads did. He loved me, but his love didn't seem consistent.
>
> Every time he left I felt rejected. When he came home I felt good for awhile, but then I resented him because he never stayed home. Perhaps that's why my relationships with men are unsuccessful. I'm never fulfilled with the men in my life because none of them stick around either. Is every man like my father?

Perhaps Susan was reliving her relationship with her

father in her dating experiences. She expected men to desert her as her father did, so her behavior tended to drive men away. Susan's pattern of relating to men in this way was painful, but it was also predictable for her, and thus she felt safe.

A father has many opportunities for emotional intimacy and for building a strong relationship with his daughter. But many men never take advantage of these opportunities. They share very little closeness with their daughters when they are young, choosing rather to become bystanding phantoms. Unfortunately, this emotional distance is maintained as daughters grow into adulthood.

A recent study indicated that 36 of 39 anorexic girls experienced withdrawal of affection from their fathers . . . upon reaching puberty.

This problem is partly due to the inability of most men to develop the emotional part of their lives. Men often don't learn how to express their feelings, creating a relational vacuum within them, a loneliness in a man's relationship with his wife and his daughter. This dilemma of loneliness men experience is aptly described by Ken Olson:

> There it is again!
> A twinge of pain?
> Forget it. It will go away.
> In the business of my day.
> I've places to go and things to do . . .
> A round of meetings with entrepreneurs.

Planes to catch and taxis to hail,
I have life by the tail.
But what is this painful wail?
From the depths of me I ache.
It greets me when I wake.
Even in a crowded room of people.
I can hear a haunting toll from a church bell steeple.
There's nothing wrong with me.
I'm a success, as anyone can see.
I—I hurt. I feel an emptiness.
This feeling, is it loneliness?
Loneliness?
I'm married with children, three.
Yet at times I feel so alone.
Maybe it's time to come down from my throne.
It's not good for a man to be alone.[2]

Does your father fit the description of the phantom father? Was he there, but not *really* there for you? Was he an emotionally detached bystander like Jeanine's father? Was he a caring but distant absentee like Susan's father? Has loneliness played a significant role in your father's lack of involvement with you? What effect has your phantom father had on your relationships with other men?

Coping with Phantom Problems

Let's consider two major, closely related problems which can plague the daughter of a phantom father: anorexia and bulimia. The overwhelming majority of victims of these eating disorders are women. It has been estimated that 90 to 95 percent of all anorexics, and 95 to 99 percent of bulimics, are female. Some women shift back and forth between both disorders. The devastating effects of these problems include permanent disability and even death.

Where does the phantom father fit into a daughter's eating disorders? Many other factors are involved in these disorders, but a woman's relationship with her father is often tied into her problem. Not all daughters of phantom fathers will develop eating disorders, of course. But a recent study indicated that 36 of 39 anorexic girls experienced withdrawal of affection from their fathers (which they perceived as the withdrawal of love) upon reaching puberty. Dr. Margo Maine, who conducted the study, feels that anorexic behavior may be a girl's attempt to postpone adulthood by remaining "Daddy's little girl."

Research also shows that bright, high-achieving young women from middle- and upper-class families are at greater risk of anorexia and bulimia than other women.[3]

Some fathers are very loving and involved with their daughters while they are little girls. But when their daughters reach adolescence, some fathers feel insecure about relating to them as young women, so they withdraw their affection. Add to this sudden coldness a father's high expectations for his daughter's achievement and you have the right ingredients for the development of an eating disorder. In anorexia and bulimia, food is no longer used as a source of fuel, but for emotional purposes. For the daughter who feels unloved, food, or abstinence from it, often becomes a way to cope with distressing feelings of inadequacy and pressure.

If your father affectionately communicated love and acceptance to you, he probably did so by following four basic guidelines in his relationship with you. Consider sharing these guidelines with your husband. They will be beneficial to him in his relationship with your own children

1. Self-esteem is built through encouragement, not pressure.

Pressure does not build self-esteem; it eventually tears it down. Colossians 3:21 states: "Fathers, do not provoke or irritate or fret your children—do not be hard on them or harass them; lest they become discouraged and sullen and morose and feel inferior and frustrated; do not break their spirit" (*AMP*).

It is all too easy for a young girl to condemn herself for being too fat, too skinny, too tall, etc. But when her father contributes to her negative thinking, either verbally with his critical statements or nonverbally by withdrawing from her, he damages her self-image. Dr. Maine says, "A father's distance contributes to low self-esteem. If he is unavailable to provide the feedback the girl needs regarding her self-worth, he leaves her more sensitive to the negative impacts of the culture, like the drive for thinness, appetite control and the view of emaciation as beautiful."[4] Under negative pressure, some girls feel that the only way they can gain attention is by doing something drastic.

A number of women have told me that, whenever they talk with their fathers, one of the topics which always comes up is their weight: "Aren't you a little thinner?"; "You've lost some weight. Great!"; "Are you gaining a bit of weight? Oh, you look fine, but I was just curious." I wonder if questions or comments like these are really necessary.

A father's compliments about who his daughter is and what she does, and his expressions of delight and joy for her companionship, will go far to build her self-esteem. Letting a daughter accomplish what she wants to accomplish is part of this process. And letting her enjoy what she has accomplished without pushing her toward greater achievement is vital.

A daughter needs unconditional male approval, especially from her father. This means helping her accept herself and believe in her attractiveness whether she meets his expectations or standards for attractiveness or not.

2. Inner qualities are more important. What a father thinks and feels about the opposite sex will be reflected in the way he responds to his own daughter. Many fathers estrange themselves from their daughters because they value a woman's physical appearance over her inner qualities. If a father overemphasizes outward beauty and the perfect shape, his daughter, who may not look like a movie star, feels that she cannot please him. A father must accept his daughter's physical appearance and focus his attention on encouraging the development of inner qualities, especially biblical qualities.

3. Teasing or pressure about diet can be dangerous. When a father becomes too involved in his daughter's eating habits, he may blow out of proportion the importance of attention to diet. Food is a basic ingredient of life. But overemphasizing diet turns eating into an emotional power tool, either as a punishment or a reward. Even a father's playful teasing about eating can be taken too seriously by his daughter. Such teasing may implant thoughts of inadequacy in a sensitive daughter's mind. But downplaying the importance of food diminishes its power in the father-daughter relationship.

4. Proper information dispels fear. A father can be the source of balanced, healthy information for his daughter about life, food and self-esteem. A father can assist his daughter in countering the overemphasis on physical beauty in our society. He can help his daughter refute the belief that a woman must always please others. The best way for a father to impart this idea is by not insisting that his daughter always please him and by letting her know that he loves her even when she doesn't.[5]

Out of Reach, Out of Touch

I remember seeing a cartoon which showed a little girl going from one parent to the other, trying to get their attention. But both parents were involved in other things, telling her they were too busy to listen to her. In the last frame the little girl comments to the reader, "My life is one big busy signal."

Perhaps you can identify with her complaint. Was your father approachable or too busy? When you went to him, did he accept you, listen to you and respond to you? Sadly, many daughters shake their heads no on those two questions. Phantom fathers are too busy, too tired, too preoccupied or just unavailable.

One of the greatest gifts a father can present to his daughter is to be approachable. Approachability involves communication at a level where your dad is open, nondefensive, interested and responsive. Approachability requires tenderness and sensitivity to hurt or feelings of insecurity. It means being a companion. Approachable fathers listen carefully to what a daughter may have difficulty verbalizing. He listens not only with his ears, but with his eyes and his heart as well. He practices Proverbs 18:13: "He who answers a matter before he hears the facts, it is folly and shame to him" (AMP). This kind of attention prepares a young girl for her role as a woman and helps develop her ability to respond to significant males in her adolescent and adult life.

Gordon MacDonald shares the following experience from his own life in his book, *The Effective Father*:

The effective father whose ear is open and whose wisdom makes him able to accept his children as they are, adds a final quality to his reputation for being approachable. Call it flexible response. To use another telephone analogy, he doesn't put his kids on "hold."

It was the middle of the night when Kris called my name. I heard her first "Daddy!" immediately and sprang out of bed and down the hall to her room. She was in distress. There had been a bad dream, and Kris was having a rough time sorting out what was real and what was part of the dream.

Why had she called her father? Because her instinct somehow told her that when equilibrium is in jeopardy, fathers can help restore balance. Her young mind had set up a pattern of responses to uneasy situations: call for Dad; he knows how to make upside down things turn right side up again.[6]

If a daughter has an approachable father in her early years, she will need to erect fewer defense mechanisms in her life. But if she receives a harsh response when seeking her father—such as criticism, rebuff or rebuke—she will tend to make excuses for her behavior, project responsibility for her actions onto others or be fearful of taking risks.[7]

It's interesting to discover that men tend to be more open emotionally with their daughters than with their own wives, even though this openness is rather limited. Michael McGill, in his book, *The McGill Report on Male Intimacy*, indicates that men reveal more of themselves in every dimension—public, private and personal—to their daughters than to their siblings, closest friends, sons or parents. But men also often misrepresent themselves in what they share with their daughters, more so than in any other relationship. What they share may be as much fiction as fact, which means that their apparent intimacy is a loving lie. Some fathers argue that they don't really lie to their daughters, they just let them believe some information about their daddy which isn't true.

For example, some men want their daughters to believe that they are great successes in business and that they can handle just about anything. A father may have numerous motives for this grand deception. He may bend the truth "for her own good," hoping to create in her the image of him as a white knight who will protect her. He may want his daughter to see him as bigger than life because that's how he sees himself. But these lies are discovered in time and the false image is shattered. As a daughter matures, she discovers that her parents are far from perfect. Some daughters go along with their fathers' deception and see little harm in perpetuating it. But others have the opposite reaction. Here's what three daughters said:

> None of us knows what Daddy is really like, but we've all played along with him for so long that I think even Mom has stopped caring whether we know the real him or not. I don't think it matters much now. Maybe it would have if we had got it all straightened out early on, but now we all know our roles too well to try to change.
>
> Papa's so easy to fool, if you just let him think you see him the way he wants you to. My sisters and I can get anything we want from him that way. The funny thing is, he thinks we have the super-honest relationship. It's a joke, really.
>
> My father and I would get along just fine if he

would be real with me, but instead he insists on being this "big daddy" type that I know for a fact isn't real. He's just another small-time businessman in town. Why can't he admit that? I refuse to participate in his charade the way Mom and Annie do—why should I? How can you get close to someone who isn't honest with you? I won't go into all of it here, but there are some things I know about my father that are so far from the way he wants us to think he is that it's like two completely different people. Because he won't be straight with me about who he really is, I can never trust him. I'm not sure I'll ever be able to really trust any man, and I have my father to thank for that wonderful outlook.[8]

Did you make a similar discovery about your father? The discovery that Dad is not all he makes himself out to be is a shock for many daughters. And often if the daughter confronts her father with the way things really are, he becomes defensive and withdraws. But he doesn't need to. Such a confrontation can lead to a more open, honest and close relationship.

Models of Weakness

Some men are phantom fathers because they present a weak model of what a man's role is all about. They may be weak in many situations outside the home. For example, a father may not be a good provider for some reason. If a daughter perceives that this problem stems from her father's irresponsibility, poor judgment, impulsiveness, laziness, passivity or unwillingness to take risks, she may feel that he has little or no strength to offer her. This weakness in itself could color a daughter's perception of men in the future.

If a father is wishy-washy, ineffective or unassertive in dealing with people, his daughter comes to believe that she won't be able to depend on him or lean on him. If he is morally weak, a daughter learns that she can't count on him to assist her in developing her own moral guidelines.

Often a daughter notices that her father is weak or subordinate in his interaction with her mother. For example, perhaps her father goes along with his wife on a wide range of decisions, including where they live, their choice of friends, how leisure time is spent, where they go when they go out, etc. She may see him lose every argument or give in to her mother again and again. She may notice that everything her mother wants is fine with him. He shows no strong desires or preferences. Such apparent weaknesses build into the daughter a lack of confidence in her father and suggest to her that all men are spineless.

There are other ways by which a father's manifested weakness around his wife can affect his daughter more directly. Your father may have punished or scolded you, not because *he* was upset, but because your mother pushed him to do so. Or a weak father may punish his daughter because he is angry with his wife, but was afraid to take out his anger on her. The daughter becomes the scapegoat. If your father was weak in his relationship with your mother, you have likely given up appealing to him to intervene in your interactions with your mother. He just wouldn't help you, so you have given up trying.

A daughter usually does not seek the counsel of a weak father because he is so ineffective in managing his own life successfully. Other daughters learn to avoid discussions with their weak fathers on some topics because they can never get definite answers from their fathers, or the answers are shallow. A weak father causes his daughter to fear that she may overwhelm him with her emotional or intellectual needs. She ends up feeling that she is too much for her father. Disillusionment sets in and her respect for him erodes.

The Impact of a Weak Father

What are the results of a relationship between a weak father and his daughter? If a daughter grew up with a weak father, she may be quite comfortable with a weak man in her life. She was her father's rescuer as a child and adolescent. As she grows into adulthood and leaves her father, she considers her rescuing mission to be incomplete. She is attracted to men who need her. I like the way Howard Halpern describes it:

> There are many ripples emanating from the turbulent interactions that pass for relationships between a weak father and his offspring. Perhaps you are locked into a pattern of finding enfeebled "father figures" and then dedicating yourself to overlooking their weakness or to forever propping them up to look strong . . . . I have seen women with weak fathers unerringly and repeatedly select, out of a large number of men who cross through their life space, men who are little boys in many ways— perhaps alcoholics, drug addicts, love addicts, failures in careers, inept at earning a living and unable to assert themselves except perhaps in a little boy demandingness, tantrums, and sulkiness. [9]

Unfortunately, the daughter of a weak father feels it is her duty to "fix" the weak men in her life like she tried to fix her father. She wants to build a strong man to lean on, someone who will finally fill the role her weak father couldn't or wouldn't fill. But she keeps finding new things to fix in her men because, if she completed the task, she wouldn't know how to handle a strong man. If she does run out of flaws to correct, she feels let down, disappointed and even victimized. And her search for a man to complete begins all over again. The daughter must finish the task of raising her own father—or some other man in his place—to manhood. Many women engage in this fruitless pursuit for years. The men they select are really child-men, as described by Dr. Dan Kiley in his book, *The Peter Pan Syndrome.*

*If you are the victim of a weak father
. . . you must abandon the idealistic
hope that you can ever make
him strong.*

Some daughters of weak fathers are fortunate to find strong men with whom they can identify. A strong man can turn the tide for a woman whose primary masculine model, her father, was weak. Her new model of strength can be a source of learning and guidance for her, filling the void created by a weak father.

Breaking the Rescuing Pattern

If you see yourself in the description of the rescuer, you can break out of this pattern by first of all recognizing the effect a weak father has had on your life. You must admit to yourself that there were ways he failed you, ways he can never atone for. Also, breaking the pattern means choosing to see your father from a much wider perspective. You must try to discover as much as possible about his life, development and experiences as a child in order to understand better why he is the way he is. In the process you may discover some of his strengths which you have overlooked because of your feelings of disappointment and hurt.

If you are the victim of a weak father, there are two responses you must give up. First, you must abandon the idealistic hope that you can ever make him strong. Second, you must relinquish any vindictiveness toward him for his failures and shortcomings. If you do not let go of your false hope and vindictiveness, you will continue to be controlled by your father's weakness. Are you surprised by that statement? Many women are. They don't realize that they have been in bondage to their fathers all these years.

If your father is still alive, begin to relate to him on the basis of the strengths in his life. Refuse to engage in responses which emphasize his weaknesses. This means you will need to ignore some of his behaviors, respond to other behaviors in new ways and reinforce your responses to his positive behaviors. You won't be changed overnight, but at least change will become a possibility for you.

The effects of your relationship with your weak father must be carefully considered as they impact your relationships with other men. I have talked with many women who were stuck in the repetitive cycle of rescuing weak men as they tried to rescue their weak fathers. Some came to me wondering if there was more to life than performing rescue missions without ever getting any time off. If you are continually trying to rescue weak men, it is time to break your addiction to this kind of person. The pattern will never be changed just by changing men in your life. You must change your beliefs, attitudes and ways of responding to these men. It is important to remember that change is possible through the power and presence of Jesus Christ.

Wilma was a 37-year-old woman who had spent 20 years trying to rescue weak men. The comments she shared with me were very insightful:

> I spent all that time choosing men who in their own way were weak like my dad. About two years ago I told myself that I was not going to be frightened off again by a man who had ideals and strengths. I knew what the weak men were like, so I decided that I had nothing to lose by dating the opposite type.
>
> I met George at a singles group at our church. At first I was fearful because he seemed together emotionally. I couldn't find too many weaknesses as we dated. I discovered he was the type of man that you could rely upon, and I didn't need to rescue him in any way. He treats me as an equal and we have learned to help each other when there is a need. What a relief! It feels as though for the first time in my life I'm free!

Reading *The Peter Pan Syndrome* and *The Wendy Syndrome,* by Dr. Dan Kiley, will be beneficial to you as you strive to break the rescuing pattern. Also, it will be helpful for you to talk with your husband or a close male friend about your past tendencies and how they affect your present relationship.[10]

Notes

1. Elizabeth Fishel, *The Men in Our Lives* (NY: William Morrow and Co., 1985), adapted from pp. 142, 144, 159 and 161.
2. Ken Olson, *Hey Man, Open Up and Live* (NY: Fawcett, 1978), pp. 147-148.
3. Margo Maine, adapted from her paper, "Engaging the Disengaged Father in the Treatment of Eating Disordered Adolescents," presented at the annual conference sponsored by the Center for the Study of Anorexia and Bulimia, New York, November 1985.
4. Ibid.
5. Nicky Marone, *How to Father a Successful Daughter,* (NY: McGraw-Hill, 1988), adapted from pp. 270-279.
6. *The Effective Father,* by Gordon MacDonald. Published by Tyndale House Publishers, Inc. © 1977 Used by permission. All rights reserved.
7. Ibid., adapted from p. 133.
8. Michael E. McGill, *The McGill Report on Male Intimacy* (NY: Harper and Row, 1986), pp. 122-123. Used by permission.
9. Howard Halpern, *Cutting Loose* (NY: Bantam Books, 1977), pp. 55-56. Used by permission.
10. Ibid., adapted from pp. 45-62.

SEVEN

Why Does Daddy Still Run My Life?

"I can't relate to all this talk about fathers who were absent or uninvolved in their daughters' lives," Claire admitted to me. "My father was *over*involved in my life. I would have given anything for some freedom from my father when I was growing up. In fact, he's still overinvolved in my life: dictating, smothering, controlling. My sisters and I call him 'Little Hitler' behind his back. I need a break from that man."

We hear so much today about the uninvolved father that the suffocating influence of the overinvolved father is often minimized. In some cases these fathers are applauded for their "deep concern and sacrificial involvement" in their children's lives. But I've talked to many women like Claire who complain, "Dad never let me grow up; he always made my decisions for me" or "Daddy always took care of me then and—I hate to admit it—he still takes care of me now. He jumps in even when I don't ask him for help." It's usually the mother who tends to be overinvolved in the child's life. But some daughters come from families where both parents are strongly controlling. And in other homes the mother is distant, so the father makes up the deficit by getting deeply involved.

Fathers and Their Children

Children want attention and involvement from their fathers. Studies indicate that, by the age of 20 months, children are as attached to their fathers as to their mothers, but significantly more responsive to play initiated by their fathers. In a report to the Society for Research in Child Development, Alison Clarke-Stewart stated that in three-way play activity—child with mother and father—children of both sexes are more involved, cooperative, excited and interested when playing with their fathers. Over 70 percent of the children participating in the study preferred their fathers as their playmates.[1]

Other research shows that fathers who are responsible for child care at least 60 percent of the time in their homes, as opposed to 22 percent in the average home, positively affect their daughters' lives. The major benefit she receives from this extra care is a greater belief in her ability to influence her own destiny and the external events which influence her life.[2]

But there is a down side to a father's relationship with his daughter. Research reveals that fathers give more time and attention to their sons than to their daughters. One study noted that men show a preference for sons over daughters by nearly four to one![3] In another study, two researchers observed fathers at home when their babies were three weeks old and then three months old. The observers noted that the fathers with sons were more deeply involved with their babies than the fathers with daughters. The fathers with sons touched their babies more, showed them more toys and looked at them more often than did the fathers with daughters. Fathers with sons were also more involved with their infants at feeding time. Other studies performed in the U.S. and Sweden show that fathers are more willing to maintain involvement with "difficult" boys than with "difficult" girls.[4]

A girl may be hurt, angry or resentful when her brother receives preferential attention from their father. She wishes her father was more involved in her life. She begins to wonder if she is as important to her father as her brother. She may feel emotionally abandoned by a father who apparently likes her brother more.

Another area in which a father treats his sons and daughters differently is in his hopes, dreams and expectations for his children. Two thousand mothers and fathers were asked, "What kind of person do you want your son or daughter to become?" The fathers responded with much higher expectations for their sons than for their daughters. For example, fathers desired their sons to be ambitious, hard-working, responsible, intelligent and strong-willed. All they desired for their daughters was that they be attractive, kind, loving and unselfish.

Fathers didn't specify that their sons should have good marriages and should be good parents, but these qualities were listed for their daughters. In their lists for sons, fathers listed only one desired relational trait: protective. But for their daughters they listed ten: nurturing, caring, sensitive, sweet (whatever that means!), understanding, flexible, compassionate, self-sacrificing, gentle and warm. Many fathers don't realize that these relational characteristics are as important for men as for women. First Peter 3:7 states: "You husbands likewise, live with your wives in an understanding way" (*NASB*). Living in an understanding way involves many of the relational traits fathers only hoped for in their daughters. Scripture calls men to develop characteristics which some fathers would label feminine.[5]

In the study I have conducted with women in premarital counseling over the past ten years, one of the questions I asked was, "What is/was your father's goal for your life?" Of the hundreds of women interviewed, 80 percent said their fathers just wanted them to be happy. Very few daughters related that their fathers' held high career or achievement goals for them. One response I received seemed to combine a healthy balance of goals: "My father always wanted me to work in the public school system as a school counselor. I guess he still wants me to do this, but mostly he wants me to do what makes me happy and fulfilled. He has always wanted me to keep myself attractive in all areas of my life in order to attract a wonderful man with positive qualities and to have a successful marriage and raise good children."

Some fathers come from deprived homes and backgrounds. These men often react to their upbringing by being very protective of their daughters. They don't want their little girls to suffer as they did. They may pamper or overprotect their daughters, expressing little confidence in their abilities. The protective father is often able to get away with his overinvolvement under the guise of being a loving father. Sometimes he becomes so dependent on his daughter in the process that he finds it difficult to release her when she wants to move out or marry.

Teaching Helplessness

Most fathers have no idea how great an impact their preference for sons has on their daughters. This impact was dramatically demonstrated in an interesting study by Jean Block. Parents were videotaped as they helped their children solve a difficult puzzle. When fathers assisted their sons with the puzzle, they did so by emphasizing problem-solving skills and focusing on the boy's performance and success. But when fathers sat down with their daughters over the puzzle, they were not task-oriented, but relationship-oriented. They joked with their daughters, encouraged them and rescued them. They actually put pieces of the puzzle together without their daughters asking for help! For fathers and sons, the puzzle was a problem to be solved. For fathers and daughters, it was a game to be enjoyed.

On the positive side, the behavior of these fathers demonstrates their willingness to protect their little girls. But on the negative side, their responses illustrate the subtle message which many fathers convey to their daughters: "You need Daddy's help because you are not capable of doing it yourself." By their actions, these fathers unwittingly inject their daughters with what is now called "learned helplessness." These girls grow up feeling weak and inferior, needing their fathers to fix everything for them. Girls like this often end up being dominated by their fathers—and other father figures—in adulthood.

Fortunately, many girls are more independent and self-reliant, resisting the learned helplessness some fathers foist on them. I have a daughter like that. Right from infancy Sheryl wanted to do things herself and wasn't too keen about being rescued when she was having problems. She became proficient in fishing and other sports at an early age, and by the time she was five she was accompanying me on deep sea fishing trips and handling her own fishing outfit. On her second trip out she decided that she wanted to catch the live anchovies out of the bait tank, put them on the hook and toss the line into the water all by herself. Much to my surprise that day, she landed three large barracuda and fought a six-foot shark until it broke the line. (To this day she claims that *I* cut the line!)

Sheryl continued to progress in her fishing ability by mastering fresh water fishing. When she was eight years old, she started her own fish cleaning business at the ranch where we were vacationing in Grand Teton National Park in Wyoming. Much to the chagrin of some of the boys she dated, she not only knew more about fishing but out-fished them as well!

Learned helplessness . . . is a trait which some fathers teach and reinforce in their daughters by rescuing them from problem situations.

However, I remember one fishing trip when Sheryl was helpless—or at least appeared to be so. When she was 15 we went out deep sea fishing for a half day with a group. As soon as the boat stopped, Sheryl was the first person to cast a line into the water. She hooked into a good-sized calico bass right away, reeled it to the side of the boat and then just stood there looking as if she didn't know what to do next. I was about to tell her to pull it over the side when she shot a warning glance my way which communicated, "Don't say a word, Daddy." In only a few seconds I understood. A good-looking, 17-year-old deck hand approached her, eager to assist an attractive girl with her fish. We've had some good laughs over Sheryl's momentary "helplessness." She continues to fish to this day, and she fishes well.

Sheryl's helplessness that day was not the learned helplessness which many girls inherit from their fathers. She has always been self-assured, willing to try new things for herself. Her adventurous spirit led her to develop a business designing and creating hand-painted earrings.

Learned helplessness is not a female trait; it is a trait which some fathers teach and reinforce in their daughters by rescuing them from problem situations. Boys learn to experiment until they find solutions; many girls only learn to rely on Daddy for solutions. Fathers tend to believe that their daughters are more delicate, weaker and less attentive than their sons. And when a father continues to rescue his daughter, she also begins to believe that she is incapable of success without his intervention. By and large, our society has perpetuated the learned helplessness which fathers often convey. Thankfully, there are some changes occurring which allow girls and women to develop and express their capabilities.[6]

I was impressed with a suggestion to fathers from a teacher of gifted children. She urged fathers to encourage their daughters with behavior which communicates:

> I believe that you are perfectly capable of handling any situation that arises. I am here if you need me, but I will rely on *your* judgment, rather than my own, to determine if and when my help is needed. I will not jump in prematurely to rescue you and diminish your achievement.
>
> You know there will be times when you will feel frustrated and anxious, lonely and scared as you cope with the hardships that will be unique unto whatever path you choose to walk. I will love and support you

as you walk your path, but I will not save you from its lessons. I will not trespass on your right to grow, to make mistakes, and to learn the lessons inherent in them. I will not trespass on your right to autonomy.[7]

Did your father rescue you as a child? What kinds of rescuing behaviors did he use? Does your husband tend to rescue your daughters? If so, how? Talk with him about this issue to make sure that neither of you are guilty of teaching your daughters learned helplessness.

The Dominated Adult Daughter

When you were a child, your father was significantly more knowledgeable and capable than you were. It was natural for him to use his adult wisdom and strength to guide your life and help solve your problems. Now that you are an adult, you don't expect him to treat you like a child anymore—but he does. If you asked him why he still tells you what to do, he may answer, "Because I love you and want the best for you." In reality, he probably still feels entitled to the parental power he exercised over you when you were young. He cannot admit that you are now a capable adult. He tries to dominate you with advice you don't ask for and don't want. His messages start with words like, "You should . . . " or "Why don't you . . . . " Even his questions are not really questions, but instructions in disguise. You feel like you don't have the freedom to give your own response. He still wants you to "do what Daddy says," not what you desire.

One 27-year-old woman told me dejectedly, "Dad walked into my house and, within the first hour, made seven disparaging comments about the way I kept the place. He also made four changes in my decorating scheme—and he didn't even ask my permission!" It's hard to deal with a father like this since he uses his daughter's anxiety and his concern to control her. On the surface, some of his requests seem legitimate. But they are often masked by his hidden agenda: control. And if she does not comply with his suggestions, he heaps on the guilt by showing concern, disappointment or hurt.

There are several ways by which adult daughters are dominated by their fathers. Let's consider some of them.

Dominated by default. Isn't it strange that, when your father gives you an order as his adult daughter, you still feel that you will be sent to your room or denied privileges if you don't obey him? I've talked to women in their 50s who still say, "How high?" when their fathers say, "Jump." Women like this are dominated mainly because they default control to their fathers when they don't need to.

Brenda, a woman in her mid-40s, surprised me one day by saying, "Norm, my father still knows what's best for me. I know it sounds like I'm a perpetual child, but I still respond to what Dad says. I guess I get some satisfaction out of the old saying, 'Father knows best.'"

I had worked with Brenda in counseling for some time, so I felt safe in asking her some penetrating questions. "Brenda, could it be that saying no to your father would be the same as saying you know what's best for your life, thus taking away the comfort and security of relying on your father? Is there any possibility that making decisions for yourself uncovers some personal feelings of insecurity? Perhaps you feel inadequate in some areas of your life and, as much as you'd like to be in charge, decision-making feels risky to you. Your dominating father just happens to be a handy cover-up for your weakness."

The look on Brenda's face—a look of shock that only a

realization of the truth can produce—confirmed that I had struck a vital nerve. With her secret exposed, Brenda had to face it—and she did. Over the next few weeks a new pattern of adult behavior began to form in her.

Does Brenda's story remind you of yourself? Have you been using your father's dominance as camouflage for your own weakness? Like Brenda, you can face your weakness and overcome it.

Dominated by negative reaction. June, a 40-year-old home-maker, shared with me her struggles with doing too much by being overly accommodating and submissive to people. I suggested that she cut back or cancel some of her activities. But she answered, "You mean say no to someone after I've already said yes? That would be changing my mind. I couldn't do that."

"What's wrong with changing your mind?" I asked. "What kind of message are you afraid it will convey?"

"When you change your mind and fail to follow through," June answered, "that means you can't be trusted and you're not responsible."

"What gave you that idea?" I pressed. "Who taught you that?"

"My father always changed his mind and backed out on responsibility," she said, "and I vowed I would never be like my father."

"So your father is still controlling your life, isn't he?" I stated pointedly.

June was silent for several seconds, looking a bit stunned at my comment. "I guess I never realized that he was influencing me like that," she admitted.

Like June, many adult daughters are dominated by their fathers even when they determine to live the oppo-site of what their fathers exemplified, taught or stood for.

Their negative reaction to their fathers shows that they are still controlled by them. Has this been your experience also?

Dominated by weakness. Some parents have learned that they can control their adult children with their personal problems or physical weaknesses. Deanna's father, who wasn't in as poor health as made out to be, called Deanna every Friday and asked if she would be near his neighborhood during the weekend. If she said no, he would reply in a wounded tone, "Well, I guess I'll have to let the cleaning go for another week. But that's all right. I can get by."

Sometimes a father's disabilities are real, but his demands are unreal. He uses his weakness as a lever to exert control over his sympathetic daughter. Has your father used this ploy on you? Have you been able to meet your father's genuine needs without letting his exaggerated needs dominate you?

Dominated by finances. Some fathers control their daughters with their wallets. For example, a man insists that his daughter carry on the family business, volunteering to pay for the education she will need to prepare her. He exercises additional control by boasting to family and friends how wonderful it is that his daughter will be following in his footsteps.

But his daughter feels trapped. She doesn't particularly want to carry on her father's business, but she's afraid that she won't make it financially on her own. She wants to be free from Dad's influence, but she also needs an education to make her own dreams come true. Stepping out on her own would probably mean that her father would withdraw his financial support. She's in a real bind!

Did your father ever use finances as a means to control your life? Does he do so now?

Dominated by fear. Some men are addicted to power and control. Like despots, they tend to dominate those around them, including their families, by fear. A tyrannical father believes he owns you. You are his possession. He's the type of man who, as Howard Halpern describes, burdens you with a list of commandments which he has burned into your mind: "I'm your father and I'm more important than anyone else"; "My needs and wants get met first"; "I deserve respect, thanks and gratitude from you"; "You go along with my rules or else."[8] The "or else" doesn't go away when this father's daughter becomes an adult. He merely changes it to provoke more fear.

Some daughters defy or rebel against their tyrannical fathers, especially during adolescence. The anger and hatred of these women often hardens into cold aloofness or ignites into blazing defiance toward their fathers and all other men: dates, husbands, employees, employers, teachers and friends. The dominated daughter longs for a warm, loving, accepting man in her life. But every man she meets is either dominant like her father or weak in comparison to him, provoking the same response: angry rebellion. She fights the same battle with other men she fought with her father: the battle for survival.

Did your father dominate you with fear? If so, what "or elses" did he use to control your behavior? Do you still fear him? Why or why not?

The Father-dominated Family

If your family was dominated by your father, how did the other family members respond? Did they more-or-less accept domination or was there an overt or underground rebellion against your father?

The family which is dominated by a controlling father lacks closeness and intimacy. Family members are afraid of transparency and vulnerability because the father might exploit their openness to control them further. And the dominating father can't tolerate the vulnerability that closeness requires. Besides, if his dominance is successful in making the family function, who needs to draw close? Power is primary to the dominating father.

A dominating father also affects the family's communication style and problem-solving techniques. There is little or no negotiating in this family. Thus you may have grown up not learning how to compromise in a healthy manner or to differ agreeably.

A controller is quite skilled in using anger to control and manipulate those around him. He tends to hold high and unrealistic expectations for others and is known as a nit-picker. He creates fun at others' expense, often resorting to put-downs and sarcasm. He rarely apologizes and is skilled at making excuses for his mistakes. He projects blame on others and few dare to disagree with him. No matter what he does, he must come out on top; he must win. Everything in the family must be geared around him. He keeps everybody else on egg shells. (For additional information on controllers, read Kevin Leman's book *The Pleasers: Women Who Can't Say No and the Men Who Control Them* [Revell].)

Expressing feelings in a father-dominated family is risky business. He often disapproves of the expression of anger, hurt, sadness, depression, joy or delight. A daughter's feelings of resentment toward her father must be kept hidden. At the same time, a dominating father can produce feelings of guilt in his family members. He may say, "Someone has to take charge around here. If I don't do it, nothing will get done. I have to be the responsible one since the rest of you are irresponsible."

Connie's story illustrates the typical results of a dominating father in a family. At age 15, Connie was referred to a psychiatrist because of excessive fears which had been plaguing her since she was 13. At first she was just afraid of heights, then she became fearful in any room holding more than a few people. For several months prior to her referral Connie refused to leave her bedroom, eating all her meals there. Connie's entire family was called in as part of her evaluation.

The family interview was completely dominated by Connie's father, a successful surgeon. He asked all the questions, ordered members of the family to answer, cut off their responses at will and changed the subject frequently. He was openly sarcastic and demeaning to his wife. The father's leadership style was open and overbearing domination.

Connie's mother was passive and subdued, sitting close to Connie and holding her hand. During Connie's withdrawal her mother had entered into a coalition with her, spending much time in Connie's room. Jeff, the 19-year-old son, was also caught up in the family dilemma. He was sullen and visibly angry. He had not made his grades in college and had been unable to find a job for six months. Jeff's father was displeased at his son's performance and had threatened to kick him out of the house. He seemed to make a point of defying his father with behavior that displeased him.

During the individual interviews it was apparent that each member of the family was in great pain. Connie was obviously fearful and depressed, crying through her interview. She seemed abnormally dependent on her mother.

Jeff was angry and critical of his father. He seemed unaware of any connection between his frequent failures and his anger at his father. Connie's mother was quiet, depressed and spoke about deep feelings of loneliness. Connie's father was angry and bitter about the way his family was turning out. He felt responsible to "carry" them all and felt burdened about his inability to do so. He saw his domineering, controlling behavior as a response to the other family members' inadequacies. [9]

For the dominated family, life often contains more pain and misery than joy and satisfaction. But even a family like Connie's can be helped. With time and extensive counseling family members can give up destructive patterns of interaction and discover new ways of dealing with life and each other.

An interesting and famous illustration of a dominating father is the story of Edward Barrett, the father of poet Elizabeth Barrett Browning. According to Victorian standards, Mr. Barrett was considered a loving and benevolent father. But he was also a power-hungry, domineering father, feeling that he owned a divine right to be so. He encouraged his daughter's writing as a girl, but also made her an invalid so that she would always be dependent on him. Elizabeth felt both love and constraint from her father.

Mr. Barrett forbade his children to marry. But, despite her father's protests and threats, Elizabeth became the first of his children to break the shackles, marry and leave home. She continued to write to her father, but he rejected her and denied her existence. Just before he died, Mr. Barrett sent a packet of Elizabeth's unopened letters to her husband. And when her father died, Elizabeth collapsed from untold grief at her father's final and utter rejection.

This may be an extreme case, but countless daughters have told similar stories of domination and rejection.[10]

Many daughters surrender to their dominating fathers rather than fight them. They learn to be pleasers and eventually end up feeling like victims. "I emotionally sold myself out to my father," Helen told me. "I tried to fight him a few times, but his harsh verbal attacks were too strong. In time I learned that I could count on him when I needed him—if I let him dominate my life. That's why I feel like I sold out to him. I felt used and abused emotionally. And I wonder what I can do now to break that pattern with him and with other men I relate to. Is there any hope?"

Your memories of your father and your life with him can either be a beneficial learning experience or a controlling influence in your life.

Helen has asked a good question: Is there hope? Can the effects of the past be changed? The answer is good news: Yes, yes, yes!

How Do You Feel About Your Father?

In these last few chapters we have talked about fathers who never fulfilled their roles, either by being uninvolved, overinvolved or gone. Whether your father filled his role or not, you have strong feelings about him. What are those feelings? I asked a large group of women in their 20s and

30s to describe their feelings about their fathers. I have listed here two groups of responses. As you read them, consider these questions: Which group do you identify with most? How might your future be impacted by your feelings toward your father? If you are the parent of a daughter, how do you want her to feel about her father? How does she feel about him at this time?

Your memories of your father and your life with him can either be a beneficial learning experience or a controlling influence in your life. How do you think this first group of women viewed their experiences with their fathers?

I generally feel rather negative about my father because he's so disappointed and angry over my decision not to live according to his life-style. I resent his disapproval and rejection of my life goals.

I love my father, but I worry about his physical, spiritual and mental well-being. I also feel guilty for not spending more time with him, but I do find it hard to be around him when he's drunk.

I love my father and appreciate the things he has done for me. But I'm also angry about the way he treats Mom and the way he's handled his own life. I feel pity toward him because he won't take control of his life.

I have mixed feelings. My relationship with him hasn't been easy since I was eight years old. I rejected him as a teenager and it's taken a long time to redevelop any type of relationship. It's hard to get excited about a relationship that takes so much effort, but I'm learning that it's worth it.

I'm not sure how I feel about him. Our relationship to this point has been kind of distant. He seems more like an acquaintance than a father.

My feelings are incredibly mixed. On the one hand, I have great respect and admiration for him. On the other hand, I've never been able to fully resolve my fear of him. My heart aches when I think about how far apart we are.

I love him, but we don't have a father-daughter relationship. I feel sad that he isn't loving or forgiving or close to me emotionally.

I regret being so afraid of my father throughout my childhood.

Over the past 25 years I have heard many women in counseling express similar responses about their fathers. Often a woman's relationship with her father is one of the primary reasons she is seeking counseling. But other women have had more positive experiences. Perhaps you can identify with some of their feelings about their fathers:

I love him and respect him. I am so grateful that he really tried to be the best father he could be. It was difficult for him, having come from another country and being raised by abusive parents. He was strict, but we always knew he loved us. In the next few years our relationship will probably change as we both grow older. I pray that we will both accept the change gracefully.

I loved my father very much. He had a very special ability to make each of his children feel that they were very special.

I love him very much even though I don't always understand him.

I can count on him. I *know* he loves me. I do wish he would take better care of himself. I love and respect him.

I care about my father. He has always provided for me and cared for me. Over the past few years he has become more open with his feelings and we have been able to hug each other and tell each other that we care. We play tennis each week and this has helped nourish the love between us.

Dad is one of the best things to happen to me. I can always turn to him and know I will be heard. I am grateful for our relationship. I also feel fortunate, since I have talked with other women whose father-daughter relationships were pitifully lacking in so many ways.

I love him very much. I listen to his opinions and value them because of the kind way he shares them and because his ideas help me consider possibilities I've overlooked.

In the past it has been popular to lay at the feet of our parents the burden for some of our own problems. When evaluating your parents' success, keep several factors in mind. First, every parent comes into his or her role as an amateur. Second, every parent is imperfect in fulfilling his or her role. Third, every parent brings into his or her parenting role all the imperfections of how he or she was raised. You have a choice between being bound by your parents' failures and deficiencies or accepting your past and moving on with your life. You can choose to be responsible for how you feel and respond positively to life, or you can choose to blame your parents for your problems and thus perpetuate their influence in your life. You can choose to live in the past and let the past determine who you are today, or you can choose to learn from the past but live in the present. Consider what Lloyd Ogilvie says:

> The Christian life begins when we are released from the prisons of our own making. The love of the cross unlocks the prison doors of memory. The past is forgiven and the future is open to new possibilities . . . . The past can be neither a source of confidence nor a condemnation. God graciously divided our life into days and years so that we could let go of the yesterdays and anticipate our tomorrows . . . . We are liberated to accept and love ourselves as loved by the Lord. This unshackles our relationships.[11]

"So if the Son sets you free, you will be free indeed" (John 8:36).

Notes

1. William Woolfolk and Donna W. Cross, *Daddy's Little Girl* (Englewood Cliffs, NJ: Prentice-Hall, 1982), adapted from p. 20.
2. Nicky Marone, *How to Father a Successful Daughter* (NY: McGraw-Hill Publishers, 1988), p. 88-90. Original research from Norma Radin, "Childrearing Fathers in Intact Families: An Exploration of Some Antecedents and Consequences," paper presented to study group on the role of the father in child development, social policy and the law, University of Haifa, Israel, July 15-17, 1980, as referenced

in D. Ross Parke, *Fathers,* (Cambridge, MS: Harvard University Press, 1981).

3. D. Ross Parke and D.B. Sawin, "The Family in Early Infancy: Social Interactional and Attitudinal Analyses," in Frank A. Pederson, ed., *The Father-Infant Relationship: Observational Studies in the Family Settings,* (NY: Praeger Publications, 1980).

4. E. Redina and J.D. Dickerscheid, "Father Involvement with First Born Infants," *Family Coordinator,* 25:373-379 (1976); A.M. Frodi, M.E. Lamb, M. Frodi, C.P. Hwang, B. Forsstrom, and T. Corry, "Stability and Change in Parental Attitudes Following an Infant's Birth into Traditional and Nontraditional Families," unpublished manuscript, University of Michigan, 1980, as referenced in Parke, *Fathers.*

5. Marone, *How to Father a Successful Daughter,* adapted from p. 91-93.

6. Ibid., adapted from p. 95.

7. Ibid., and Lois Hoffman, "Changes in Family Roles, Socialization and Sex Differences," *American Psychologist,* 32:649 (1977).

8. Howard Halpern, *Cutting Loose,* (NY: Bantam Books, 1977), adapted from p. 66-67.

9. Jerry M. Lewis, *How's Your Family?* (NY: Brunner, Mazel, Inc., 1979), adapted from p. 125-126.

10. James J. Rue and Louise Shanahan, *Daddy's Girl, Mama's Boy,* (NY: Bobbs-Merrill Co., 1978), adapted from p. 18.

11. Lloyd John Ogilvie, *God's Transforming Love,* (Ventura, CA: Regal Books, 1988), p. 71; Ogilvie, *God's Best for My Life* (Eugene, OR: Harvest House Publishers, 1981), p. 1.

EIGHT

Was My Family Healthy?

Darcy was 19 and a junior in college. She came into the counseling center because she was bothered by the amount of contact she was getting from her father, even though he lived 1,500 miles away. She said: "Dad calls me every other day to get advice or to complain about mother. He tells me things he should have shared with mother over the years. I've probably received more attention from him than from my mother or any of the other kids. I thought that when I went away to school I wouldn't have to be this involved with my family. But it hasn't changed. Why has this happened? And how is it going to affect me later on?"

Mary was a perfectionist. Her dress was impeccable and everything about her was precise. It was difficult for her to relax because she felt like she was always on display. She told me that her parents were divorced when she was four. When her mother remarried several years later, Mary found out that her stepfather saw her as a "necessary nuisance"—that's what he called her. He was a cold, rigid workaholic. Mary asked me, "Do you know why I am such a perfectionist? It's true there are some benefits to perfectionism, but at times I wonder if there isn't a better way to live. Why am I this way?"

In most cases, a dysfunctional family is the product of a dysfunctional husband-father.

I hear stories like these from women almost every day. They come into the counseling center, they write letters to me, they call me on the phone and they talk to me at seminars. These women wonder why they respond to life as they do. They wonder why their fathers behave as they do. They wonder if there is a correlation between the way they were raised and the way they behave now. And they wonder if they can change their behavior.

The Home That Shaped You

There are many factors which combine to make us who we are. You are the product of your family birth order, your neurological structure, your interactions with your mother, father, siblings, etc. But the atmosphere of your home, and especially your relationship with your father, had a significant impact on shaping your identity and behavior.

You are fortunate if you were raised in a healthy home. These families are called functional families because they function effectively and productively. Functional families display many of the following positive qualities:

- The climate of the home is positive. The atmosphere is basically nonjudgmental.
- Each member of the family is valued and accepted for who he or she is. There is regard for individual characteristics.
- Each person is allowed to operate within his or her proper role. A child is allowed to be a child and an adult is an adult.
- Members of the family care for one another and they verbalize their caring and affirmation.
- The communication process is healthy, open and direct. There are no double messages.
- Children are raised in such a way that they can mature and become individuals in their own right. They separate from Mom and Dad in a healthy manner.
- The family enjoys being together. They do not get together out of a sense of obligation.
- Family members can laugh together, and they enjoy life together.
- Family members can share their hopes, dreams, fears and concerns with one another and still be accepted. A healthy level of intimacy exists within the home.

Do these characteristics reflect the home in which you grew up? Evaluate the health of your family by rating each trait on a scale of one (never evident) to ten (always evident). No family scores tens across the board. But if your score averages seven or above, you were fortunate to be raised in a functional family.

Don't feel bad if your scores are low. The general health of your family of origin was something over which you had little or no control. Furthermore, you are not the prisoner of your upbringing. The goal of this chapter is to help you understand the negative impact of your less than perfect family—and especially your less than perfect father—on your life today. Understanding why you are the way you are is the first step to positive change.

The contrast between a healthy family and an unhealthy family is evident in the responses of six women, all in their 20s, to the following question: "How do you feel about your father?" What do their responses tell you about the health of their respective families? How would you characterize each woman's relationship with her father?

Robyn: I am regretful that I feared my dad so much while I was growing up. Even today I state my feelings to him in such a way as to meet his approval or gain his acceptance. I feel that I could have learned so much if he had been more open to what I was going through as a child. I love him immensely, and I feel happier now that I see him starting to grow.

Lynn: My feelings are incredibly mixed. On one hand, I respect and admire him. But on the other hand, I have never been able to resolve my fear of him. My heart aches when I think of how far apart we are. I feel that he doesn't really know me, not the real me. I feel incompetent, ignorant and indecisive when I am around him. I wish I didn't.

Beth: I feel numb now. It used to be a love-hate relationship, but that tore me apart.

Jill: In the last two years I've become much more comfortable with my father in open communication. I think of him as a friend. Our relationship is, and always has been, on a more equal basis than father-daughter.

Teri: My father has been my best friend for as long as I can remember. I've always been able to talk to him, and I love him very much.

Renee: I love him to death, and I appreciate how well he's done in our home and in his career. I am very proud of him and wouldn't want anyone else to be my "Daddy."

A Family Off Course

If the characteristics of a healthy, functional family above are the opposite of your family experience as a child, you probably come from a dysfunctional family. Dysfunctional families lack much of the acceptance, openness, affirmation, communication, love, caring and togetherness of healthy families. In most cases, a dysfunctional family is the product of a dysfunctional husband-father, one who failed to occupy a healthy, positive role due to uninvolvement, domination, illness/death, desertion/divorce, etc. If you are from a dysfunctional family, this discussion will help you better understand yourself and your relationship with your father. Also, it will help you determine the characteristics you want to develop in your own home.

Several times a year I travel on airplanes. So far I've always arrived at my intended destination, mainly because the plane stayed on course. If a plane strays off course just a few degrees, I might end up in Cuba instead of Washington, D.C. The longer a plane travels off course, the farther it wanders from its destination.

A dysfunctional family is a family that has strayed off course. Though they probably don't think of it in these terms, every newly married couple wants to build a functional family. Their "destination" is a loving, healthy, happy relationship between husband and wife, parents and children. But many little things can go wrong in families: feelings get hurt, needs and expectations go unmet. If these minor midcourse errors are not corrected, greater problems arise: love and acceptance are withheld, "me" and "mine" take priority over "us" and "ours." Soon the prospective "happy family" is far off course and exhibiting the characteristics which are described in the following pages.

When a family gets off course, a child's needs for security, warmth, guidance and encouragement go unmet. What about you? How did your father meet your need for security? How did he guide you? What about your need for warmth? How did he encourage you? Or did your needs go unmet in your family? Many children from dysfunctional families are thrust into adulthood feeling empty and incomplete, afraid and unable to trust because their needs went unmet. And when you don't feel secure in yourself, you look for some type of security outside yourself. You're always trying to fill up the empty space inside. It's this constant quest to have needs met which leads people to create or adopt compulsive or addictive behavior patterns.

Imagine that your life is represented by a cup. When you were born your cup was empty. You had a lot of needs which had to be met. If your family was healthy, most of your needs were met, and when you reached adulthood your cup was full or almost full.

But if your family wasn't healthy, your cup may only be a fourth, a sixth or an eighth full. You entered life with needs which your father and your family should have met, but didn't. The lower the level in your cup, the more you tend to try to fill it from the outside, often with compulsive or addictive behavior. Many adult emotional problems exist simply because people are carrying cups which have never been full. All of us have problems at some time in our lives. Some of us handle them in healthy ways, some of us don't. It depends upon the level in your cup.

Any family can become dysfunctional for a period of time, especially during a crisis when we don't function at our normal levels. Often someone else—such as a pastor or a counselor—must step in and help us function until we are back to normal. But in a dysfunctional family the crisis is perpetual and the roles of the family members are usually constant.

One of the best descriptions of a dysfunctional family comes from Sara Hines Martin:

> It can be a home where a parent or grandparent is chronically ill or mentally ill or a home where a parent is emotionally ill, including chronically depressed. It could also be a home where one parent dies and the surviving parent is so overcome by grief he or she is unable to cope with the parenting tasks; a home where physical and/or sexual abuse takes place; a home where suicide has taken place; a home where a child was adopted; and the rigidly religious home. (This last category surprises many people because nothing is specifically done, as in the other categories. This type of home produces similar dynamics because children are not valued for themselves but are raised by rigid rules. The father, if a minister, may neglect his family while carrying out his work. The children can get the feeling they must make the parents look good in the eyes of the community.) In summary, these families focus on a problem, addic-

tion, trauma, or some "secret" rather than on the child. The home is shame-and-blame based.[1]

The phrase "shame-and-blame based" is one of the best descriptions for this type of home. It is totally contrary to the pattern of love and acceptance presented in the Scriptures.

Characteristics of the Dysfunctional Family

There are several telltale traits of families which stray off course. I want to share ten of them with you. How many of these exist in a family and how often they occur reflect how far the family has strayed from healthy family norms. As we consider these characteristics, and as you evaluate your past and present families, focus on your father. If any of these characteristics existed, what was his part in the drama? You may want to respond to each characteristic and its description with one of the following statements: "This trait describes my family well"; "I'm confused about how this trait applies to my family"; "This trait doesn't describe us at all"; "I'm angry at . . . "; "I'm hurt because . . . "; "I'm sad because . . . "; "I have some real questions and doubts about this one. I need to talk to someone about my past."[2]

1. Abuse. Abuses which characterize the dysfunctional family can include physical, emotional or sexual injury or neglect. Abuse may be blatant, such as one family member striking or screaming at another. It can be subtle, as when one person ignores another. Abuse can also be vicarious, such as the inner pain you suffer when observing the abuse experienced by your mother, brother or sister.

One form of abuse which is often overlooked because

it leaves no visible scars is emotional abuse. Here are some examples:

- Giving a child choices which are only negative, such as saying, "Either eat every bite of your dinner or get a spanking."
- Constantly projecting blame onto a child.
- Distorting a child's sense of reality, such as saying, "Your father doesn't have a drinking problem, he just works too hard and he's tired."
- Overprotecting a child.
- Blaming others for the child's problem.
- Communicating double messages to the child, such as saying, "Yes, I love you" while glaring hatefully at the child. The child will believe the nonverbal message and be confused by the words.

Were you the victim of emotional abuse from your father? Remember: The painful residue in your life from emotional abuse can be cleared away. Healing *is* an option.

2. Perfectionism. Are you surprised that perfectionism is a characteristic of a dysfunctional family? It's rarely considered an unhealthy symptom, but it is a common source of many family problems, especially in Christian homes. After all, isn't the challenge of the Christian life to be perfect as God is perfect? Not really. We are called to live a life of excellence, which is attainable, not perfectionism, which is unattainable. Expecting perfect behavior from spouse or children, even in a Christian family, is living in a world of unreality.

A perfectionistic father conveys his standards and expectations through verbal rebukes and corrections, frowns, penetrating glances, smirks, etc., which continually imply, "It's not good enough." He lives and leads by oughts, shoulds and musts. These are "torture words" which elevate guilt and lower self-esteem. A father who constantly overfocuses on defects in a critical way erodes his child's self-image. The child begins to believe that he is hopelessly substandard, and he carries this poor self-image with him into adulthood.

Did your father have perfectionistic tendencies? If so, what evidences do you see in your present life?

3. Rigidity. Dysfunctional families are characterized by unbending rules and strict life-styles and belief systems. Life is full of compulsions, routines, controlled situations and relationships, and unrealistic and unchallenged beliefs. Joy? There is none. Surprises? There are none. Spontaneity? There will be none—unless it is planned! If your father was a rigid family head, you probably heard him say something like, "There are two ways to do it: the wrong way and my way. We're doing it my way."

To what extent was your father rigid in his family leadership? How did he show it? How has his rigidity affected your adult life?

4. Silence. Dysfunctional families operate by a gag rule: no talking outside these walls. Don't share family secrets with anyone. Don't ask anyone else for help if you're having a problem. Keep it in the family. After all, what would people think if they knew you didn't have it all together?

If your father invoked the gag rule at home, you probably grew up thinking that you have to handle all of your problems by yourself. It's difficult for you to ask for assistance or advice. You are hesitant to ask others to pray for you or counsel you.

5. *Repression.* You may have grown up in a family where emotions were controlled and repressed instead of identified and expressed. Emotional repression has been called the death sentence of a marriage. Anger, sadness, joy and pain which should be expressed among family members are buried. The name of the game is to express the feelings which are appropriate instead of what you really feel. Deny reality and disguise your true identity by wearing a mask. But when you bury your true feelings alive, some day they will explode in your face.

Emotions are a very important part of life. Like a pressure valve, they help us interpret and respond to the joys and sorrows of life. Clogging the valve by repressing or denying feelings leads to physical problems such as ulcers, depression, high blood pressure, headaches and a susceptibility to many other physical ailments. Repressing feelings can trigger overeating, anorexia and bulimia, substance abuse and compulsions of all types.

People repress their feelings to make them go away. But, of course, they don't. They fester and grow, looking for a means of expression. Some people stay excessively busy so they won't hear the screams of their feelings which are just waiting to burst through. Repressed feelings cause people to do things they don't intend to do, like yelling at the children, abusing pets or bursting into tears at a party.

Repressing your feelings is like putting a waste paper basket in the hall closet, setting it on fire, closing the door and leaving the house. You don't know what the outcome will be. The fire could extinguish itself, or it could spread and burn down the house. But by repressing your feelings, you are no longer in charge of them. You don't know when or where they will pop up. Functional families identify, express and deal with feelings as they occur. Dysfunctional families bury feelings and then become the victims of all the pressures and explosive problems which result.

How did your original family, especially your father, deal with emotions? Use the lists of feelings below to help you identify how well your family expressed emotions. Place your father's initials beside each feeling you remember him expressing in the context of your family. Place your initials beside the feelings you expressed. Then do the same for the rest of your original family:

embarrassed	loving	worried	jealous
accepted	disappointed	guilty	affectionate
fearful	apprehensive	sad	morose
hurt	inferior	inadequate	rejected
mistrusted	depressed	afraid	frustrated
joyful	lonely	defensive	happy
elated	shy	angry	disgusted
grumpy	cheerful	jolly	glad
amazed	festive	edgy	shy

What did you learn about your father, yourself and other family members? Was the expression of any of these feelings forbidden in your home? If so, who said so and why? Are there any feelings which are difficult for you to identify and express at this present time in your life?

6. Triangulation. Triangulation relates to the communication process in the family. In triangulation, one family member uses another family member as a go-between. Father tells his daughter Sally, "Go see if your mother is still angry at me. Tell her I love her." Sally compiles with his request. But Mother retorts, "Tell your father to get lost!" How does Sally feel about getting caught in the middle? Perhaps she feels like a failure. She let her father down. Perhaps she fears that her mother is angry at her.

If triangulation is a regular pattern in a family, the child feels used and becomes involved in problems which she should not be part of. She becomes a guilt collector, experiencing feelings she doesn't need and cannot handle. Did you experience triangulation in your family? Did your father and mother, or any of your siblings, use you as a go-between?

7. Double messages. A wife asks her husband if he loves her. "Of course I do," he says as he gulps his food while reading the newspaper. Then he spends four hours in front of the TV and goes to bed without saying one more word to her. His words say, "I love you," but his actions say, "I don't care about you at all." It's a double message.

A young girl puts her arms around her father and feels his back stiffen as he subtly tries to pull away. Both say, "I love you," but she also hears his body language saying he doesn't like being close to her. It's a double message.

Double messages abound: "I love you"/"Don't bother me now"; "I love you"/"Get lost"; "I need you"/"You're in my way"; "Yes, I accept you"/"Why can't you be more like Susan?" Double messages are confusing, especially for the child. Did you hear them in your family?

8. Lack of fun. Dysfunctional families are typically unable to loosen up, let go, play and have fun. They are overbalanced to the serious side of life. Their mottos are: "Be serious"; "Work hard"; "You are what you do"; "Play is a waste of time." When members of a dysfunctional family engage in play, it usually ends up with someone getting hurt. They don't know when to stop. And humor is used as much to hurt as to have fun.

Did your family have fun together? Did your father promote fun or stifle it? How did your father express humor?

9. Martyrdom. Dysfunctional families display a high tolerance for personal abuse and pain. Children hear their parents preaching that others come first, no matter what the personal cost. Children see their parents punish themselves through excessive behaviors such as drinking too much, overworking, overeating or exercising too hard. Children are challenged: "Tough it out, son; big boys don't cry"; "You aren't hurt, Jane, so quit that whimpering—or else!" They see themselves as victims, pleasers or martyrs.

As adults, these people learn to steel themselves against weakness by denying themselves pleasure or advantage, and by suppressing their true feelings. Some martyrs actually pride themselves on how much they can bear before the pain becomes intolerable. Some, in the name of Christian humility, endure destructive responses from others which deny their value as children of God. God never asked us to live like this. Being a martyr is not a spiritual gift! It's a distortion of self-denial.

10. Entanglement. The members of a dysfunctional family are emotionally and relationally entangled in each other's lives. Individual identities are enmeshed. There are no clear cut boundaries between each member. Everybody is poking his nose into everybody else's business. Mom makes Dad's problems her problems, Dad makes the kids' problems his problems, and so on. If one family member is unhappy, the whole family is blue, and everybody blames everybody else for the state they're in. It's as though the whole family is sitting together on a giant swing. When one goes up, the others go up. When one goes down, the others go down. Nobody thinks or feels for himself.

Does this description remind you of your family? Did you have difficulty establishing your own identity because your family was so entangled in your life? How has this characteristic affected your adult life?

It's true that your past, especially the family in which you were raised, has molded your adult life and directs much of your present behavior. But the negative influences of a dysfunctional family are not irreversible. The molds of your past can be cracked open and broken apart, as we shall see in the chapters ahead.[3]

Parenting in a Dysfunctional Family

The father plays a critical role in keeping his family on course. Similarly, if a family strays off course, it's primarily because the father has strayed from his role of being a positive, healthy model and guide for his children. A father may falter in his parenting in a number of ways. We will look at three of the most common.

Family rules. Do you remember some of the rules your father established for you as a child or adolescent? What was his purpose in "laying down the law" and what did it accomplish in your life? Ideally, family rules are designed to protect and guide the child, to help her develop responsibility and to help her discover her identity. Your parents determined family rules based on certain rules for parenting which they brought into their roles. If their parenting beliefs, concepts and rules were healthy, then the rules they set down for you were probably healthy and helped you develop in a positive way. But if their parenting rules were off course, their guidelines for you were probably off course. Instead of helping you develop positively, they may have contributed some beliefs, attitudes and behaviors to your life which you as an adult would rather abandon than maintain.

Some fathers are more interested in a child's unquestioned, consistent obedience than in her development as a person. In his view, a good child is one who is seen and not heard, and who speaks only when spoken to. The parent operates from a set of parenting rules similar to many which I have heard from numerous parents over the years. Frankly, these rules carry a degree of poison. They do not parallel the guidelines for parents in the Word of God. Do you remember hearing any of these rules stated or implied in your parents' home?

1. Parents have the privilege of dominating and controlling a dependent child.
2. Only parents have the right to determine what is right and wrong. They are the ultimate source of knowledge.
3. If a mother or father becomes angry with a child, the child is responsible for those feelings.
4. A child must always protect and shield his or her parents from others. Sharing what occurs in the home is not permitted.
5. A child's feelings have no place in the home.
6. It is important to break a child's will as soon as possible.[4]

The following dysfunctional attitudes are often passed from generation to generation with no one breaking the unhealthy pattern:

1. Eliminate hatred by forbidding it.
2. A child should respect parents simply because they are parents.
3. Love can be produced through teaching a child feelings of duty.
4. Children do not deserve respect because they are children. They must wait until they are older.
5. Teaching a child to obey makes the child strong.
6. Too much self-esteem is harmful to a child. It can lead to pride.
7. The best way to learn to be unselfish is by developing a low-degree of self-esteem.
8. It is wrong to respond to a child's needs.
9. Expressing tenderness to a child is detrimental to the child's development.
10. The best way to prepare a child for the realities of life is by being stern, cold and severe.
11. The way a child behaves is better than the way she really is.
12. Pretending to be grateful is better than sharing your true response.
13. Your body is "dirty."
14. Strong feelings are unhealthy.
15. If you offend your parents or God, neither will ever get over the offense.
16. Parents are always right.[5]

Parents who believe these statements will invariably pass them on to their own children. And young children believe their parents. That's their security. That's why a child tends to assume blame for any physical, sexual, mental or emotional abuse from her parents. If a young child accepted and understood her parents' inadequacies, she couldn't handle the intense anxiety. So when they do something bad to her, she naturally thinks it's her fault because she can't bear to believe that her parents are bad.

Did you idealize your father despite the fact that some of his parenting rules were dysfunctional? Have you perpetuated some of his rules in your present family without realizing it?

Abandonment. Another way a father or mother contributes to a dysfunctional family is by abandoning a child. Parents abandon children in numerous ways. Did any of these happen to you or to someone you know?

Abandonment occurs when one or both parents . . .

- actually physically leave the child.
- fail to display their emotions for the child.
- fail to affirm the child's expressions of emotions.
- fail to provide for the child's developmental dependency needs.
- abuse the child physically, sexually, emotionally or spiritually.
- use the child to fill their own unmet dependency needs.
- use the child to meet the needs of their marriage.
- act shamelessly.
- deny or hide from the outside world their shameful activities so a child must cover up for them in order to keep the family in balance.
- fail to give a child time, attention and direction.

When parents abandon a child in one or more of these ways, the natural roles of parents and child are reversed. The parents, through immaturity and irresponsibility, become the children. And since she has no one to take care of her, the child becomes a parent. She must take care of herself *and* her parents. This unfortunate role reversal leaves many children feeling alone and alienated. [6]

Shame. Some of the rules your father imposed and some of the ways he abandoned you may have left you with a feeling of shame about yourself. Shame is one of the most depressing, disturbing and deadening responses to life. Shame prevents you from accepting yourself. If you are the product of a dysfunctional family, the likelihood of shame in your life is quite high.

> *Some of the rules your father imposed and some of the ways he abandoned you may have left you with a feeling of shame about yourself.*

Shame flaws the real you so that just trying to be yourself is painful. So in order to survive the pain you develop a false self, a defensive mask which is used to hide from yourself and others all the pain and loneliness you feel. And if you wear the mask long enough, you forget which is the real you—the mask or what's under it. So many times I have heard counselees cry, "I don't even know who I am. I have no identity." And most of them are women.

The effect of shame is graphically stated by John Bradshaw:

> Shame is like a hole in the cup of our soul. Since the child in the adult has insatiable needs, the cup cannot be filled. As grown-ups we can't go back as children and sit in Mom's lap or have Dad take us fishing. And

no matter how hard we try to turn our children, lovers and spouses into Mom and Dad, it never works. We cannot be children again. No matter how many times we fill the cup—the hole remains.

Shame fuels compulsivity and compulsivity is the black plague of our time. We are driven. We want more money, more sex, more food, more booze, more drugs, more adrenalin rush, more entertainment, more possessions, more ecstasy. Like an unending pregnancy, we never reach fruition.

Our diseases are about the things of everyday life. Our troubles are focused on what we eat, what we drink, how we work, how we sleep, how we are intimate, how we have orgasm, how we play, how we worship. We stay so busy and distracted that we never feel how lonely, hurt, mad and sad we really are.[7]

Shame has often been confused with guilt. John Bradshaw says that there is a significant and profound difference between shame and guilt. Guilt says, "I've done something wrong"; shame says, "There is something wrong with *me*." Guilt says, "I have made a mistake"; shame says, "*I* am a mistake." Guilt says, "What I did wasn't good"; shame says, "*I* am no good."

Have you entertained any of these feelings of shame? Was shame a prevailing feeling in your relationship with your father?"[8]

Perhaps as you read this chapter, you realized for the first time that you have come from a dysfunctional family and have been victimized by rules, abandonment or shame. You may feel sad, angry or even bitter that your family has contributed so much to your problems and struggles as an adult. I urge you not to look backward in anger, but to look forward in hope. You cannot change the past or any of the behavior which you wish could be different. Focus your energies on forgiving family members for the past and on building positive, healthy relationships for the future.

Notes

1. Sara Hines Martin, *Healing for Adult Children of Alcoholics* (Nashville, TN: Broadman Press, 1988), adapted from p. 34.
2. John Friel and Linda Friel, *Adult Children* (Hollywood, FL: Health Communications, Inc., 1988), adapted from pp. 71-75.
3. Ibid., adapted from pp. 77-79.
4. Adapted from Alice Miller, *For Your Own Good* (NY: Farrar, Straus and Giroux, Inc., 1983), p. 59, and other sources.
5. Adapted from Miller, *For Your Own Good*, p. 60, and other sources.
6. John Bradshaw, *Bradshaw on: The Family* (Hollywood, FL: Health Communications, Inc., 1988), adapted from p. 3.
7. Ibid., adapted from pp. 4-5.
8. Ibid., adapted from pp. 1-2.

NINE

Dysfunctional Roles: Do I Have One?

"What role did you play in your family drama?" I asked.

"I beg your pardon," Eve replied with a questioning look.

"What role did you play in your family drama?" I repeated. "As you were growing up you probably played a role or combination of roles in your interaction with your family. Your role was not your true self, but an identity you took on, or were forced to play, in order to get along in your dysfunctional family. People usually continue to play their roles as they move through adult life. I'm wondering what role you played?"

Eve was still a little puzzled. "My role? I guess I'm not quite sure. Perhaps you had better explain those terms to me so I can decide."

Playing Your Part

Like Eve, you probably grew up relating to your father, mother and siblings through a role you played. This is especially true if you grew up in some kind of dysfunctional family. Your role was your mask, your way of coping with the pain of not having your needs fully met by your father and other family members. If you didn't receive recognition or affirmation for who you were, you took on a role which garnered you the attention you needed.

As you read through the list of roles I shared with Eve, keep in mind that each family member usually occupies a different role from everyone else in the family. What role was played by your father? your mother? your sisters and brothers? What role did you play in the family drama?

The Doer. Janet came up to me at a family camp and complained, "The only way my family made it to camp is because I took care of every last detail for all five of us. I made sure they had their clothes ready and that every item was packed. It's always this way. I just wish my husband and children would take some responsibility for themselves and appreciate what I do for them. I'm tired of doing, doing, doing for people." But the next summer Janet and her family were back at camp. She must have forgotten what she told me the year before, because she repeated her lament almost word for word. She was still doing for others.

The doer is a very busy individual who provides most of the maintenance functions in a family. Also called the responsible one, she makes sure that the bills are paid and that people are fed, clothed and chauffeured. These tasks need to be completed even in a functional home, but the doer uses just about all her time and energy to do them. Her family's motto is: "Give it to her and it will get done."

The doer has an overdeveloped sense of responsibility which drives her. She receives satisfaction from her accomplishments because family members like what she does and, in one way or another, they encourage her to "keep it up." Often doers like Janet feel tired, isolated, ignored and used. But the recognition she receives for what she does keeps her going. Sometimes the doer is also the enabler in the family.

The doer in most families is one of the parents, often the mother. Janet is a good example. Who was the doer in your home? How did the other family members acknowledge him or her in that role? How did your father relate to the doer role in your family?

The Enabler. The enabler provides the family with emotional and relational nurture and a sense of belonging. She is the peacemaker, preserving family unity at all costs. Her main goal is to avoid conflicts and help everyone get along. Her actions are driven by two fears: She is afraid that family members cannot survive without each other and she is afraid of being abandoned.

Enabling behavior usually happens so gradually that the enabler is often unaware of it. She is constrained to do whatever is necessary to keep the family on an even keel. Unfortunately, the enabler will even excuse or defend a family member's dysfunctional behavior in order to keep peace. For example, the wife of an alcoholic may cover for him and deny that he has a problem in an attempt to hold the family together. But, sadly, enabling behavior also allows the enabled family member to continue his dysfunctional behavior.

Sometimes the enabler can be unpleasant, resorting to anger, nagging or sarcasm to get the family to do what she wants. Some Christian enablers misuse their faith in family crises. Instead of doing something constructive about a problem, they sit around waiting for God to intervene with a miracle.

Was there an enabler in your family or was this role shared by everyone in a healthy way? Did you enable your father in any way? Do you enable him now?

The Loner. This person copes with family pressures by physically or emotionally withdrawing from others. She avoids intimate contact with family members, preferring to stay out of sight, either in her room or away from the home. When she is with others she doesn't enter in much. In a sense her withdrawal fills the need other family members have for autonomy and separateness. But the way she does so is unhealthy for her and her family.

If the loner is a child, she doesn't feel close to either parent. Usually her personality is quite passive and she shows very little anger. She rarely distinguishes herself in any way and often goes unnoticed. Even her moments of accomplishment are often overshadowed by others who attract the limelight. She is the lost child, the forgotten one in the family. Many lost children grow up to be lost adults. Sadly, they never find their place in life, living entirely in denial.

Did anyone take on the loner's role in your family? If so, how did it affect the health of the family?

The Hero. Everyone seems to like having a hero around, someone whose success and achievement brings recognition and prestige to the family. The hero is addicted to pleasing others: parents, teachers, employers, God. When the family star successfully fulfills her parents' dream for her, she often accepts the dream as her own. And the acknowledgment she receives for her good deeds builds up the self-esteem of her family members.

But the personal cost for playing this role is astronomical. The hero strives for achievement at the sacrifice of her own well-being. She does not develop a well-integrated personal value system because her focus is always on pleasing others. She tends to be very critical so friendships are difficult to come by. She guards her feelings closely, because she is afraid that if her real feelings come rushing out she will be seen as weak.

Heroes are often the oldest children in their families. As such, they often become enablers by denying themselves in order to care for younger siblings in order to please their parents. But the results in adult life can be hurtful. Elaine told me that she felt like she had been a parent most of her life. Being the oldest of seven children, she was given adult responsibilities at an early age. She liked some of the responsibility and did well, but she never learned how to play as a child. Now that she is married, her husband complains that she is too serious and isn't any fun to be around. Elaine told me the story of her painful relationship while, like a true hero, displaying very little emotion.

Heroes eventually burn out because of their strenuous efforts to be good through overachieving. As the hero's external role gradually disintegrates, she begins to behave in ways that are totally foreign to her. Heroes often turn out to be the complete opposites of their assumed roles.

When did your father occupy the role of hero in your family? When did you take that role? Who was hero most of the time in your family? How did you feel about that person?

The Mascot. This person is the family clown. She brings humor into the family through play, fun and even silliness. She's always joking and cutting up, especially when confronted by difficult situations. Her fun-loving nature is a great cover for her feelings of pain and isolation. The mascot's humor brings her the attention which she is unable to gain in other areas.

Often the mascot of the family is a young child, even though I have met some adults who fit this role perfectly. Who was the mascot in your family? Is that person still occupying that role today?

The Manipulator. This person is a clever controller in the family. She learns early how to get others to do what she wants them to do. She knows how to seduce, to charm, to play sick and to appear weak. She uses every trick in the book to get her way.

Was there a manipulator in your family? How did your father respond to the manipulator?

The Critic. This person is the fault-finding negativist in the family. She always sees glasses as half empty instead of half full. The critic is characterized by sarcasm, hurtful teasing and complaining. She would rather use her energy to tear others down than build herself up. Critics are not very pleasant to be around, but some families must endure them.

Did someone in your family play the critic's role? Was your father the critic in the family? If so, how did you deal with him?

The Scapegoat. This person is the family victim. She ends up as the blame collector for the family. Her misbehavior makes everyone else in the family look so good that they can say, "If it weren't for her, our family would be all right." If the scapegoat tries to change her role, other family members are not likely to let her off the hook. As long as she's around, they have someone to blame for their own irresponsibility.

Even though the scapegoat doesn't seem to care what is going on, she is actually the most sensitive person in the family. She is especially sensitive to the hurt she sees in the family, so she acts out the stress she feels through her misbehavior. Her actions may be a cry to the rest of the family to do something about the hurtful things which are happening in the home.

When the scapegoat is a child in the family, she feels responsible for keeping her parents' marriage together. If she senses problems between them, she may misbehave to unify them in attacking her.

Was there a perpetual scapegoat in your family? Did your father fill that role in any way? Did you?

Daddy's Little Princess/Mommy's Little Man. I've heard parents refer to their children using these terms, and often they do so in fun. But in some families these terms are not harmless nicknames, but very subtle and intense forms of emotional abuse. For example, a dysfunctional father may thrust his daughter into the role of little princess as a substitute for his wife in some ways. This father is afraid of getting his emotional needs met by his wife, so he elevates his daughter to princess status and uses her to gain emotional fulfillment.

Being Daddy's little princess may make the child feel very special. But, unfortunately, she is denied her childhood because her father demands adult responses from her. The boundaries of the child are not respected; they're violated! When the child grows up, in many cases she becomes the victim of physical or emotional abuse by other adults.

In what way did you play the role of Daddy's little princess? In what way was this role thrust upon you? What have been the results in your adult life?

The Saint. This child is expected, in an implied way rather than in an explicit way, to be the one to express the family's spirituality. For example, parents may expect their daughter to go into full time Christian work. But under the pressure of conforming to this role, she may end up denying her sexuality because her normal desires seem so unspiritual. Her worth as a person becomes dependent upon following the course of action laid out by her parents.

Did anyone express this role in your family? If so, how was this person treated by other family members? Did your parents have any expectations like this for you? If so, how did you become aware of them?

A person adopts a role in a dysfunctional family as a means of defense, a way to deal with family difficulties and pressures.

It's important to remember that the reason these roles are unhealthy is because they are just that—roles. In a healthy family, no one is pigeonholed into one slot and expected to remain there the rest of her life. In a healthy family you are allowed to be yourself and your own personality is allowed to come to the forefront. Other family members encourage you to develop and express who you are. Your mother and father are united in their beliefs and values. Their children tend to be more secure since they don't feel the need to take on roles in order to keep the family in balance.

You may be wondering, "Why would anyone want to continue playing a role, especially those which are so unhealthy for the individual or the family?" It's not usually a matter of choice. A person adopts a role in a dysfunctional family as a means of defense, a way to deal with family difficulties and pressures. That role becomes part of that individual's personality. As she grows into adulthood, she continues to utilize her role to deal with problems in the world outside the family. She may realize to some extent the pain of her role, but she usually finds it easier to accept that pain than to face the world without the defensive armor of her role. Any role can be dropped, if you really want to drop it and are willing to endure the discomfort of change.[1]

Telltale Signs from the Past

Perhaps you were fortunate in that you came from a balanced, healthy family where the roles described above were minimal or temporary. But chances are you were not so fortunate, being the product of a dysfunctional family. Something happened to you growing up in that family, and it happened more than once. Each time it happened it hurt. You learned to protect yourself the only way you knew how: by playing a role. Now, as an adult, you are still trying to protect yourself. But your feeble defense doesn't work any better now than before. Instead, your life is plagued with the symptoms of unresolved pain from your childhood family.

Adults from dysfunctional families tend to develop many different symptoms as a result of what happened to them as children. It's true that some people from healthy families display similar symptoms. But most people who suffer from these symptoms can trace them to a dysfunctional family background. These symptoms resulted either from your normal defensive response to life's stresses or they grew out of, and were perpetuated by, denial of stress. Your continuing response of defense and denial allows you to endure your pain and promote the illusion that you are in control. But it's *only* an illusion. The presence of the symptoms described here is a definite sign that you are not in complete control of your life. You are still dealing with the pain and fear from your childhood family in a dysfunctional manner. You are still denying a large segment of your feelings. You are still living a facade which is creating a false basis for close, intimate relationships.[2]

You may be acquainted with the term "adult children of alcoholics." It refers to individuals who grew up in dysfunctional families where one or both parents were alcoholics. Today there are multitudes of support groups around the country which help adult children of alcoholics deal with the residual pain and ongoing symptoms of their past experiences. You may not be the adult child of an alcoholic, but perhaps you grew up suffering under another particular family dysfunction. Like the children of alcoholics, you also need to deal with the pain and symptoms from your past.

Many of the symptoms can be classified as emotional or psychological:

depression	anxiety or panic attacks
suicide or suicidal thoughts	obsessions and compulsions
addictions of any kind	low self-esteem
personality disorders	phobias
hysteria	sexual dysfunction
suspicion	intimacy problems
emotional repression	lack of concentration
passive/aggressive personality	extreme dependency

excessive anger
inability to play or
    have fun
people pleasing

low frustration tolerance
inability to be assertive
approval seeking
identity confusion

There are numerous physical symptoms as well. These can include:

chemical dependency
accident proneness
migraine headaches
constipation/diarrhea
muscle tension
ulcers, colitis and
    digestive problems

eating disorders
tension
respiratory problems
sleep disorders
TMJ

These symptoms act like demons of confusion by preventing you from experiencing your true feelings. They distort your feelings. They blunt your feelings. They hide your feelings. For example, whenever one of Tanya's family members dies, she feels the normal emotions of sadness and grief. But in Tanya's dysfunctional family, her father never allowed tears because, to him, tears were a sign of weakness. So her normal feelings became distorted into rage, an emotion her father approved because it reflects strength. Now whenever Tanya is sad, disappointed, discouraged or hurt, instead of having a good, healthy cry, she throws an angry fit. Her true feelings have been twisted. Her compulsive anger is merely a symptom of an unmet need.

That's the way it is with many individuals from dysfunctional families. The multitude of normal emotions spiral down an ever-narrowing funnel which transforms them into one or two intense emotions. You don't really feel your fear. You don't really feel your loneliness. You don't really feel your sadness or rejection. They are all funneled into anger, which manifests itself as bitterness, criticism, dissatisfaction and abuse toward yourself and everyone else.

Another major distortion of normal emotions is lust. Normal, positive feelings like tenderness, caring, empathy and closeness, when they are squelched in a dysfunctional family, are twisted and funneled into lust. The pure emotions of love lead to fulfillment; but love twisted into lust leads to emptiness. Eventually a person loses the ability to identify and to express her true feelings.

Addictive/Compulsive Behavior

There are two symptoms I would like to clarify since they occur frequently in adult children of dysfunctional homes. They are addictions and compulsions.

An addiction is an out-of-control *dependence* which negatively affects the daily function of the person in some way. There is physiological addiction, which is a dependency on substances such as food, drugs, caffeine, etc. But there are also a multitude of emotional/psychological addictions rampant in our society, such as dependencies on work, television, love, sex, stress, reading, relationships, power, sleep, cults, etc. Few of these things are wrong in themselves, but when participation in them cannot be controlled, they become addictions.

A compulsion is an out-of-control *behavior* which, ironically, gives the participant the illusion of being in control. Compulsive behavior can include excessive jogging, gambling, cleaning, spending, etc. Any good behavior can become a compulsion if the individual cannot control his appetite for it.

Christians as well as non-Christians can fall victim to addictions and compulsions. Yet Christians tend to hide their problems more than others because "Christians aren't supposed to have those kinds of problems." Sometimes we misuse our spiritual resources to cover the problem instead of seeking the proper help which can set us free.

Perhaps the best way to discover if you are the victim of an addiction or a compulsion is to examine the characteristics of addictive/compulsive behavior. Use the following list to help you determine if you have an addiction or a compulsion which is out of control and, if so, how strong that symptom is in your life. As you read through the list, think about yourself and the other significant people in your life: your father, mother, siblings, spouse and children. What kinds of addictive/compulsive behavior characterize your family? I will use the term *addictive agent* to represent all specific addictions and compulsions.

1. Preoccupation. The person is immersed in the addictive agent. She thinks about it, talks about it, looks forward to it, is distracted by it and is even unable to be herself with others because of her preoccupation. The addictive agent seems to be her primary concern in life. She is more interested in jogging, reading, watching TV, eating, etc. than being with those who mean the most to her.

2. Increased tolerance. Over time, the person develops increased tolerance for her involvement with the addictive agent. She needs more and more of whatever she is addicted to in order to achieve the desired result. The more she uses it, the less she seems to be affected by it. And the build-up of increased tolerance leads to more intense shame, guilt and remorse.

3. Loss of control. The individual promises herself that she will stop or cut back on watching TV, drinking, reading pornographic books, etc. But she is unable to keep her promises.

4. Withdrawal. Whenever the individual tries to cut back or stop, withdrawal symptoms occur, such as depression, crying, anger or irritability.

5. Secretive behavior. Guilt and shame cause the individual to be sneaky and clever in her involvement with the addictive agent. She tends to hide "the evidence" or even lie to cover her problem.

6. Denial. It is difficult for the person to admit she has a problem, so she denies it. She is often quite defensive: "I don't have a problem. I don't need to watch TV. I can turn it off at any time. It's no big deal." She rationalizes her behavior to justify her involvement with the addictive agent.

7. The yo-yo complex. Personality changes and mood swings occur in the victim of addictive/compulsive behavior. She may be angry one moment, supremely happy the next moment and then angry again. Sometimes these swings are evident to others, but frequently they are hidden so well that only the addicted person is aware of their presence.

8. Blaming. This individual habitually blames others for her own shortcomings and mistakes. Her motto is: "It's not my fault; somebody else is responsible." She blames anyone or anything that is handy: children, spouse, job, etc. She has difficulty accepting personal responsibility for her problems.

9. Mental lapses. Persons involved in chemical addictions can experience blackouts. Those involved in less harmful addictions often become so preoccupied with their addictive agent that they don't remember very well. Daydreaming is part of this process.

10. Physical problems. Depending on the addiction, affected individuals may experience headaches, ulcers, hypertension, etc.

11. Rigid attitudes. These can include intolerance of differing viewpoints, compulsiveness, all-or-nothing thinking, etc.

12. Low self-image. Personal value loss occurs over a period of time. As the addiction continues, the individual stops caring about herself. She begins to behave in ways which are contrary to her original value system.

13. Tragedy. In some of the most serious addictions and compulsions, the final result is disability or death.[3]

Some people think addictive and compulsive behavior is restricted to major problems like alcoholism and drug abuse. Many individuals do fall into these categories, but many other people are trapped in other out-of-control dependencies and behaviors, some of which are not even classified by society as addictions. All addictive/ compulsive behavior is aimed at quickly filling an inner void. But the relief is only temporary. The more a person resorts to her addiction, the less able she will be to discover the permanent healing which is also available.

As you have read through this section, what feelings did you experience? Did any memories rise to the surface?

Did anyone's face come to mind? Sometimes reading about symptoms, characteristics of addiction and compulsion, or problem families is difficult because they are all too real and close to home for you. But remember: Identifying and facing the problem is the first step to making it no longer a problem!

---

*All addictive/compulsive behavior
is aimed at quickly filling an inner
void. But the relief is only temporary.*

Reacting Instead of Responding

Another major symptom seen in individuals from dysfunctional families is codependency. Have you heard this term? Are you aware of how widespread codependency is? Do you know what it means? Melody Beattie says: "A codependent person is one who has let another person's behavior affect him or her, and who is obsessed with controlling that person's behavior."[4] The word commonly refers to a wife who doggedly stays beside her alcoholic husband thinking that she can help him. But now it describes more broadly anyone who subjects herself to a problem person.

This definition takes on greater meaning through the experiences of codependents. One woman said, "For me codependency means staying married to an alcoholic." Another woman said, "I'm always looking for someone to rescue." A thrice-married 40-year-old woman said, "For me it means looking for men with problems and marrying them. They are either alcoholic, workaholic or have some other serious problem." Still another person said, "Code-pendency is knowing that all your relationships will either go on and on the same way (painfully), or end the same way (disastrously), or both."[5]

Sometimes codependency is confused with responding out of love, kindness, concern or even righteous indigna-tion. You may be a very giving, caring, compassionate indi-vidual and want to help others in difficulty. This is a normal and natural response. But there is a difference between helping and codependency. A codependent reacts to another person's problem instead of responding to his need. In fact, the codependent often overreacts or under-reacts. Instead of measuring and controlling her responses, she allows the problems, pains and dysfunc-tional behaviors of others to dictate her actions. If they're not careful, even professional care-givers, such as doc-tors, nurses, counselors and pastors, can become code-pendents to the persons they are trying to help.

Codependency is also progressive. As the problems of those around her intensify, the codependent's reactions intensify. But, unfortunately, her reactions don't cure the problem.

When a codependent reacts she tends to express the first emotions she feels—anger, guilt, self-hate, worry, hurt, frustration, fear or anxiety. Similarly, she latches onto the first idea that pops into her head. She speaks the first words that come to her mind, often later wishing she could retract them. There is little or no thinking until after her reactionary response. Melody Beattie says:

> Reacting usually does not work. We react too quickly, with too much intensity and urgency. There is little in our lives we need to do that we cannot do better if we are peaceful. Few situations—no matter how

greatly they appear to demand it—can be bettered
by us going berserk.

Why do we do it then?

We react because we're anxious and afraid of
what has happened, what might happen, and what is
happening. Many of us react as though everything is
a crisis because we have lived with so many crises
for so long that crisis reaction has become a habit.
We react because we think things shouldn't be happening the way they are. We react because we don't
feel good about ourselves. We react because most
people react. We react because we think we have to
react. We don't have to.[6]

Remember the last statement: "We don't have to."
Later in this book we will discuss why you don't have to
react any more.

Perhaps these two chapters on dysfunctional families
have raised some painful issues concerning you and your
father that you have never considered before. Or maybe
you feel that little of this discussion applies to you because
you came from a healthy home. Either way, this information can be helpful. You undoubtedly have friends and relatives who are suffering the symptoms of having grown up
in a dysfunctional family. As Christians, we have a two-fold
ministry. First, we must minister to ourselves by inviting
the healing presence of Jesus Christ into those unsettled
areas of our own lives. Second, we must convey the hope
of His presence and healing to others who may be struggling with the pain of the past.

Notes

1. John Friel and Linda Friel, *Adult Children* (Hollywood, FL: Health Communications, Inc., 1988), adapted from pp. 54-57; Herbert Fensterheim and Jean Baer, *Making Life Right When It Feels All Wrong* (NY: Rawson Associates, 1988), adapted from pp. 32-34.
2. Friel and Friel, *Adult Children*, adapted from pp. 20-22.
3. Ibid., adapted from pp. 34-36.
4. Excerpts from CODEPENDENT NO MORE by Melodie Beattie. Copyright © 1987 by the Hazleden Foundation. Reprinted by permission of Harper & Row, Publishers, Inc.
5. Ibid., adapted from p. 28.
6. Ibid., p. 65.

TEN

Your Identity: Which Father Is It Based Upon?

The Good Self-Image

When you get what you want as you struggle for self
And the world makes you queen for a day,
Just go to the mirror and look at yourself
And see what *that* woman has to say.
For it isn't your father or mother or husband
Who judgment upon you must pass.
The person whose verdict counts most in your life
Is the one staring back from the glass.

She's the person to please, never mind all the rest,
For she's with you clear up to the end.
And you've passed your most dangerous, difficult
    test

If the woman in the glass is your friend.

You may fool the whole world down the pathway of
life,
And get pats on your back as you pass.
But your final reward will be heartache and tears
If you've cheated the woman in the glass. [1]

In my crisis counseling seminar I begin by instructing
everyone to turn to another person and identify himself.
But when I tell them they cannot mention occupations in
their introductions, it almost throws some attendees into a
state of crisis!

If I asked you, "Who are you?" what answer would you
give me? Do you know who you are? Yes, you have certain
capabilities and physical attributes. Yes, you are your
father's daughter and he was very influential in shaping
who you are. But who are you? What is your true identity
and upon what is it based? Who you are, or who you perceive "the woman in the glass" to be, will affect how you
respond to life.

You may be quite satisfied with who you are and your
identity may be clearly defined. Or you may be dissatisfied
with yourself and your true identity is fuzzy in your thinking. In this chapter you will have an opportunity to discover the basis of your true identity, to examine your
father's role in shaping it and to take practical steps toward
changing your responses to others.

The first step is to find out how you see yourself.
Before reading further, take a sheet of paper and thoughtfully answer these three questions:

1. Right at this moment, how do you feel about
   yourself?
2. Describe in detail who you are as a person.
3. What is the basis of your identity?

False Foundations

People often base their identities on false foundations. Many women today base their identity on what others have said about them in the past. A girl hears her parents say, "She never cleans her room," hears her schoolmates say, "Big nose, big nose!" and hears her teachers say, "You're just one of those slow learners." So she grows up believing that she is a sloppy, homely, stupid girl. Her identity is based on the comments of others. Those comments may not be true, but if she believes them they become true for her and she acts them out as her identity.

Most of us have a critic residing within which significantly influences what we believe about ourselves and how we respond to others.

If you have based your identity on what others have said about you, you have given those people tremendous power and control over your life. Are you sure their perceptions are accurate? Are there other people who can give you a more accurate picture of who you really are?

Many women base their identity on what they accomplish and how they perform. They believe that what they do earns them certain status ratings which can increase based on the kinds of tasks or roles they become involved in.

Some women base their identity on what they possess or own. They have an insatiable need to acquire things.

When they don't feel good about themselves they head for the mall. They struggle with the tendency to compare their possessions to what other women have.

Still other women base their identity on who they know. Unfortunately, these women end up being name-droppers who tend to be threatened by the status of others, or who become a threat to others in their quest for status.

Many women base their identity on how they feel about their appearance. They spend countless hours in front of the mirror. They change clothes several times a day and spend a lot of money on beauty aids. This woman's entire day or evening can be ruined if she *feels* unattractive. I emphasize her feelings about herself because her attractiveness is largely based on her perception of how she looks. Twenty-five people may rave about her appearance, but if she doesn't see herself as attractive, the compliments of others have no impact. Often her perceptions are based on the reactions of others, especially her father, to her appearance during her childhood and adolescence. If Daddy was stingy with his compliments, she may be especially hard on herself as well.

I like what Jan Congo has said about these false foundations in her book *Free to Be God's Woman*:

> When we contrast our appearance, our accomplishments, our friends or our possessions to others we are making a comparison based in large part on fantasy. We have never walked in the shoes of those women to whom we compare ourselves so we fantasize what it would be like. When we do this we compare our worst, of which we are most aware, to their best. And we're really comparing ourselves to a fantasy. Perhaps this is one of the reasons why soap

operas and romance novels are so popular today. We are basically dissatisfied with our existence so we vicariously live our lives through other people.

When we believe we are only worthwhile if we are beautiful, if we use the right products, if we know the right people, if we are successful or if we are financially comfortable, we are building our self-image on faulty foundations. Subtly we find ourselves looking to other "significant" people to define for us what it means to be beautiful, what are the right products to use, who are the right people to associate with, and what it takes to be financially comfortable.

When we swallow these faddish opinions, society loves us because we fit its mold. But what happens when the mold changes?[2]

Your Beliefs Affect Your Identity

What do you believe about yourself? Is your identity based on a faulty foundation? To help you find out, answer the questions below as honestly as you can:

1. Do you believe that there is something inherently wrong or bad about you?
2. Do you believe your adequacy is defined by the approval or disapproval of others? If so, who are these people? Did your father disapprove of you? If so, how does that make you feel?
3. Do you believe your adequacy is tied to how much money you make? Where did this belief originate?
4. Do you believe that you always must be right about everything to be adequate or feel good

about yourself? Do you believe that if you are wrong, you will be disapproved of or rejected?

5. Do you believe that you are inadequate because you are overly sensitive?

6. Do you believe that you are helpless and powerless?

7. Do you believe that you must please everyone in order to be worthwhile?

8. Do you believe that your adequacy is tied to how much education you've had?

9. Do you believe that your adequacy and worth are tied to how you look? how tall or short you are? how fat or thin you are?[3]

Most of us have a critic residing within which significantly influences what we believe about ourselves and how we respond to others. Your internal critic is like a condemning conscience. It operates on the basis of standards which were developed in response to the judgments and evaluations of your parents and other people you looked up to. Your internal critic is quick to point out that you don't measure up to these standards. Sometimes your critic is like an internal parent who scolds you in the same words and tone your father used. In their excellent book, *Mistaken Identity*, William and Kristi Gaultiere explain the damage your internal critic can do:

It's your internal parent that has idealistic self-expectations for you and is quick to criticize and condemn you for not being a "good enough Christian." It's the cruel perpetrator of the crime of murdering your self-esteem. It can also cause spiritual havoc in your life because it is the foundation upon which you build your God image. When you internalize negative and punitive attitudes people have expressed toward you, it's natural to expect that others will treat you in the same way. In this case the sound of God's loving voice can easily get distorted through the loud-speaker of your internal critic.[4]

When a woman has an identity problem due to false beliefs about her adequacy and a ruthless inner critic, her feelings about herself will always ride the roller coaster. So why do some women hang onto their negative beliefs about themselves? There are several reasons.

First, some have yet to discover that there is another way to live. No one has pointed out to them that their faulty beliefs are not based on facts. They need to discover in God's Word the wonderful truth about who they really are in Christ and base their identity upon what God says.

Second, some women hold onto their inadequate identity and low self-esteem as a form of self-induced punishment. They feel that the guilt and worry they suffer are forms of penance which they hope will cancel out their past wrongs.

Third, suffering through feelings of inadequacy is a good way to elicit self-pity and pity from others. But there is a price to pay. Self-pity damages an already sagging self-image and identity. Living in a state of perpetual suffering immobilizes you, keeping you from putting forth the energy to do anything constructive.

Fourth, suffering protects you from the risks of change. Some women find it easier to remain in a state of feeling inadequate than to move ahead into new experiences where they have no assurance of success. Change takes time, effort and risk, and some women would rather suffer than change.

Fifth, some women see suffering as a way to be different and bend the rules a little without losing the approval of others. People feel sorry for you and allow you greater latitude in your behavior if they know you don't feel good about yourself. If you demonstrate guilt and anxiety about your life, they will be more accepting of your behavior.

Sixth, women with low self-esteem and a fragile identity often end up sacrificing their wants and needs to others and letting others control them, thus making themselves feel virtuous. Such self-effacing behavior may help this woman feel that she is better than others. She may base her actions on a misunderstanding of the scriptural qualities of selflessness and respect for authority. And she has a built-in excuse for her failures, because it's impossible to please everyone all the time.

Furthermore, when you make other people take responsibility for making your decisions, you are relieved of a major task. It's easier to let others make decisions for you. And if the decisions don't work out, you are not responsible.

Self-sacrificing behavior is also a subtle way to control others. When you remind them how much you have given for them and how often you let them make the decisions, you can make them feel guilty and get what you want from them.

But self-sacrificing behavior leads to a number of negative results. Intimacy is lost in your relationships. It may appear as though others admire you because of what you have done for them. But true friendship and intimacy cannot exist in a relationship where one person is a controller and the other is a pleaser. Neither person is willing to be open and vulnerable. Also, the sense of security you get from abdicating responsibility to others is false. It doesn't last and you don't grow stronger through the process.[5]

I've actually had counselees become angry when they hear the negative consequences of letting others control them. They have avoided looking at the down side because acknowledging it takes away their excuses for not making significant changes in their behavior.

Time to Clean House and Redecorate

Why cling any longer to your low self-esteem and false identity when God has called you to something better? Let's consider now God's alternative for your faulty beliefs about yourself and discover how to appropriate it.

I've talked with a number of counselees who say, "I really want to get rid of some of my old beliefs about myself. They do nothing but limit me. I really think it's time to clean house."

I usually answer, "That's a good beginning, but what about the rest of the work?"

"What other work?" they ask.

"House cleaning is only half of the job," I answer. "You also need to redecorate. Some of your deeply entrenched beliefs may not be that easy to dispose of. You will need to replace them with new, accurate and positive beliefs about yourself."

It's so important that you let go of your past identity which is based on inaccurate messages about you, and build a new self-concept which is based on the unconditional love and acceptance of God. To do so, you need to decide which you value more: your old, false identity or your true, God-given identity. Once you decide which is of greater value (is there any question?), then you need to let go of one and grab for the other.

Dr. Paul Tournier compared Christian growth to the experience of swinging from a trapeze. The man on the trapeze clings to the bar because it's his security. When another trapeze bar swings into view, he must release his grip on one bar in order to leap to the other. It's a scary process. Similarly, God is swinging a new trapeze bar into your view. It's a positive, accurate, new identity based on God's Word. But in order to grasp the new, you must release the old. You may have difficulty relinquishing the familiarity and security of your old identity. But think of what you will gain.[6]

Your Perception of God

An integral element in your positive self-identity is your perception of God. If your view of God is inaccurate, your view of yourself will also be inaccurate. Ideally, your over-all response to God, based on a proper perception of Him, will be one of trust. But many women really struggle with accepting the fact that God loves them and that He is trustworthy. Instead they are angry at God, feeling that He failed to protect them or that He let them down. Intellectually they may acknowledge that God is the giver of good gifts. But emotionally they perceive Him as the giver of bad gifts. David Seamands describes the problem in this manner:

> When we ask individuals to trust God and to surrender to Him, we are presuming they have concepts/ feelings of a trustworthy God who has only their best interests at heart and in whose hands they can place their lives. But according to their deepest gut-level concept of God, they may hear us asking them to surrender to an unpredictable and fearful ogre, an all-powerful monster whose aim is to make them miserable and take from them the freedom to enjoy life.[7]

One of the main reasons people hold false perceptions of God is our tendency to project onto God the unloving characteristics of the people we look up to. We tend to believe that God is going to treat us as others do. The Gaultieres agree:

> We like to think that we develop our image of God from the Bible and the teachings of the church, not from our relationships—some of which have been painful. It's easier if our God image is simply based on learning and believing the right things. Yet, intensive clinical studies on the development of peoples' images of God show that it is not so simple. One psychologist found that this spiritual development of the God image is more of an emotional process than an intellectual one. She brings out the importance of family and other relationships to the development of what she calls one's "private God." She says that, "No child arrives at the 'house of God' without his pet God under his arm." And for some of us the "pet God" we have tied on a leash to our hearts is not very nice, nor is it biblically accurate. This is because our negative images of God are often rooted in our emotional hurts and the destructive patterns of relating to people that we carry with us from our past.[8]

Imagine a little girl of seven who has known only rejection and abuse from her father whom she loves dearly. At Sunday School she is taught that God is her heavenly Father. What is her perception of Him going to be? Based on her experience with her natural father, she will see God as an unstable, rejecting, abusing person she cannot trust.

Consider just a few ways in which your image of your

father possibly may have affected your perception of God, which in turn affects your self-image.

If your father was distant, impersonal and uncaring, and he wouldn't intervene for you, you may see God as having the same characteristics. As a result, you feel that you are unworthy of God's intervention in your life. You find it difficult to draw close to God because you see Him as disinterested in your needs and wants.

If your father was a pushy man who was inconsiderate of you, or who violated and used you, you may see God in the same way. You probably feel cheap or worthless in God's eyes, and perhaps feel that you deserve to be taken advantage of by others. You may feel that God will force you—not ask you—to do things you don't want to do.

If your father was like a drill sergeant, demanding more and more from you with no expression of satisfaction, or burning with anger with no tolerance for mistakes, you may have cast God in his image. You likely feel that God will not accept you unless you meet His demands, which seem unattainable. This perception may have driven you to become a perfectionist.

If your father was a weakling, and you couldn't depend on him to help you or defend you, your image of God may be that of a weakling. You may feel that you are unworthy of God's comfort and support, or that He is unable to help you.

If your father was overly critical and constantly came down hard on you, or if he didn't believe in you or your capabilities and discouraged you from trying, you may perceive God in the same way. You don't feel as if you're worth God's respect or trust. You may even see yourself as a continual failure, deserving all the criticism you receive.

In contrast to the negative perceptions many women

have about God, let me give you several positive character qualities of a father. Notice how these qualities, if they existed in your father, have positively influenced your perception of God.

If your father was patient, you are more likely to see God as patient and available for you. You feel that you are worth God's time and concern. You feel important to God and that He is personally involved in every aspect of your life.

If your father was kind, you probably see God acting kindly and graciously on your behalf. You feel that you are worth God's help and intervention. You feel God's love for you deeply and you're convinced that He wants to relate to you personally.

If your father was a giving man, you may perceive God as someone who gives to you and supports you. You feel that you are worth God's support and encouragement. You believe that God will give you what is best for you, and you respond by giving of yourself to others.

If your father accepted you, you tend to see God accepting you regardless of what you do. God doesn't dump on you or reject you when you struggle, but understands and encourages you. You are able to accept yourself even when you blow it or don't perform up to your potential.

If your father protected you, you probably perceive God as your protector in life. You feel that you are worthy of being under His care and you rest in His security.

Even though we tend to do so, we cannot base our perceptions of God and our feelings about ourself on how we were treated by our parents. Fathers and mothers are human and fallible—and some of them are even prodigals! Our beliefs based on childhood experiences need to be cleaned out of our minds and emotions and replaced with accurate beliefs about God based on His Word. You need to transfer the basis of your identity from your fallible father to your infallible heavenly Father. Father God is the One who is consistent in His love and acceptance. Note what the Scriptures say about Him:

- He is the loving, concerned Father who is interested in the intimate details of our lives (Matt. 6:25-34).
- He is the Father who never gives up on us (Luke 15:3-32).
- He is the God who sent His Son to die for us though we were undeserving (Rom. 5:8).
- He stands with us in good and bad circumstances (Heb. 13:5).
- He is the ever-active Creator of our universe. He died to heal our sickness, pain and grief (Isa. 53:3-6).
- He has broken the power of death (Luke 24:6-7).
- He gives all races and sexes equal status (Gal. 3:28).
- He is available to us through prayer (John 14:13-14).
- He is aware of our needs (Isa. 65:24).
- He created us for an eternal relationship with Him (John 3:16).
- He values us (Luke 7:28).
- He doesn't condemn us (Rom. 8:1).
- God values and causes our growth (1 Cor. 3:7).
- He comforts us (2 Cor. 1:3-5).
- He strengthens us through His Spirit (Eph. 3:16).
- He cleanses us from sin (Heb. 10:17-22).
- He is for us (Rom. 8:31).
- He is always available to us (Rom. 8:38-39).
- He is a God of hope (Rom. 15:13).
- He helps us in tempation (Heb. 2:17-18).
- He provides a way to escape temptation (1 Cor. 10:13).
- He is at work in us (Phil. 2:13).

- He wants us to be free (Gal. 5:1).
- He is the Lord of time and eternity (Rev. 1:8).

It is so easy to hold God responsible for our problems and how we feel about ourselves. But God is not the problem. Rather, it's our mistaken perceptions of Him that block the reality of who He really is.

What is your perception of God? What is it based upon: a parent's response to you? a significant adult in your life? what a minister told you? what the Word of God states about Him? If you have never taken the opportunity to discover a clear picture of God, saturate yourself with what the Bible says about Him. Also consider two other books which will help give you an accurate picture of God: *Knowledge of the Holy* (Harper and Row) by A.W. Tozer and *Knowing God* (InterVarsity) by J.I. Packer.

In Father God's Image

Your self-image is established on several foundations. We've already identified some which are shaky and quite changeable, such as personal appearance, performance and status. But God can solidify your foundation by providing three of your greatest self-esteem needs.

First, we all need to belong, to know and feel that we are wanted, accepted, cared for and enjoyed for who we are. How it delights a woman to have this need met in her father. But not all women are that fortunate. Even if you never felt a sense of belonging with your father, this need can be met by your heavenly Father. God wants you, cares for you, accepts you and enjoys you.

Second, we all need to feel worthy, able to say with confidence, "I'm good, I'm all right, I count." We feel worthy when we do what we think we should do or when we live up to our standards. We sense worthiness in being right and doing right in our eyes and the eyes of others. God is our primary source of worthiness. We don't need to keep striving in order to feel worthy. God declares us to be all right. As Jan Congo says, "Each of us is a divine original! We are the creative expression of a loving God."[9]

Third, we all need to feel competent, knowing that we can do something and cope with life successfully. Again, God meets this need by declaring us to be competent. Philippians 4:13 is the new measuring rod by which we are assured competence: "I can do everything through him who gives me strength."

The point here is that your self-esteem and identity are gifts from God. They cannot be earned through your achievements, nor are they based on what other people say about you, do to you or fail to do to you. Whether your earthly father helped or hindered the development of a positive identity, your heavenly Father can supply anything you lack.

Steps to a Positive Identity

It's important to have the proper beliefs and a solid basis for your identity and self-esteem. But as you are establishing that solid foundation, it is also important to behave in a healthy new way. Here are several practical steps you can begin to take which will counter previous, unhealthy ways of responding to others. You may want to summarize these on a sheet of paper and post it where you will read it often.

1. Forget guilt and worry. Remember: No matter how much guilt you carry, it won't change your past, and no matter how much you worry, it won't change your future.

Worry often becomes a substitute for planning. We spend too much time focusing on the negative when we should be planning to make changes.

2. Accept the fact that you are in process. There may be certain features or characteristics about your life that you are dissatisfied with at the present. Realize that you are still the person God designed you to be. Sure, we have mental and physical weaknesses, we experience energy limitations, and we have needs and changing emotions. You may

Gauging your behavior by the reactions of others makes you their prisoner . . . . You end up saying what you think others want you to say, being what they want you to be and doing what they want you to do.

think you won't ever be what you want to be. But God has not completed implementing His design in you. You are still in the process of being shaped into a beautiful creation. God knows what lies dormant within you, but He also loves you just as you are right now. He will also love you as you continue to grow and develop. Notice that I did not say He will love you *more*. You may think or feel that God doesn't love you as much today as He will when you "improve." Not true! God's love is unconditional. *He loves you!* And He wants you to cooperate with Him in bringing out the best in you. He wants you to cooperate in the creative process.

You can hinder your growth by asking questions like,

"What will other people think?"; "Will they like me if I change?"; "What if I don't please them as much?"; etc. But you haven't been called to make a good impression. Gauging your behavior by the reactions of others makes you their prisoner. It also robs you of your individuality and leads to "impression management." You end up saying what you think others want you to say, being what they want you to be and doing what they want you to do. It's all right to be you and to develop as God wants you to develop.[10]

3. Stop avoiding responsibilities. Are you steeped in self-induced suffering and self-pity right now in order to avoid some responsibilities? Make a list of the items you are avoiding. Then consider asking someone to help you tackle and fulfill those responsibilities.

4. Expect others to be upset. Keep in mind that any changes you make may rattle the cages of family members, friends or others. They may be a little upset with some changes and very upset with other changes. Some people just have a hard time with change of any kind. But if you mentally and emotionally give them permission not always to like your changes, you will be able to handle their responses.

5. Chart the consequences. Keep a record of what happens when you entertain negative feelings and thoughts about yourself, and when you behave negatively. Review those consequences and ask yourself, "Is this what I really want for my life? Could I possibly believe and do the opposite of what I've written here?" Instead of dwelling on your negative thoughts, feelings and behavior, focus on what God says about you and promises to you. For example, in the book of Jeremiah, God says, "Call to Me, and I will answer you, and I will tell you great and mighty things, which you do not know . . . . For I know the plans that I have for you, . . . plans for welfare and not for calamity to give you a future and a hope" (Jer. 33:3; 29:11, *NASB*).

6. Evaluate your sacrifices. Make a list of all the sacrifices you are making for others and all the decisions you have allowed others to make for you. What have these sacrifices and nondecisions done for you? What label do you give yourself whenever these occur? How will you change any of these behaviors at this time?

7. Try new activities. Make a list of some special things you have always wanted to do and places you have wanted to go, activities you feel you didn't deserve. Then ask someone to participate in these activities with you. Making such a request may be difficult for you at first since it goes against your feelings about what you deserve. But don't apologize, make excuses or give elaborate reasons. Just give it a try. After each activity, write down all your positive feelings and responses. Don't list any negative comments; only positive. Give yourself an opportunity to be and do something different.

8. Believe what God believes about you. Overcoming negative feelings, whether they stem from childhood or a current situation, will take time and effort, but change is possible.[11] The main step you must take in this process is to accept what your heavenly Father believes about you. Christian psychologist Dr. Dick Dickerson has written a paraphrase of 1 Corinthians 13 which beautifully summarizes how God looks at you. Read this passage aloud to yourself every morning and evening for the next month, then evaluate how your feelings about yourself have changed:

Because God loves me, He is slow to lose
   patience with me.
Because God loves me, He takes the circumstances
   of my life and uses them in a constructive
   way for my growth.
Because God loves me, He does not treat me as
   an object to be possessed and manipulated.
Because God loves me, He has no need to impress
   me with how great and powerful He is because
   He is God. Nor does He belittle me as His
   child in order to show me how important He is.
Because God loves me, He is for me. He wants
   to see me mature and develop in His love.
Because God loves me, He does not send down
   His wrath on every little mistake I make of
   which there are many.
Because God loves me, He does not keep score
   of all my sins and then beat me over the head
   with them whenever He gets a chance.
Because God loves me, He is deeply grieved
   when I do not walk in the ways that please
   Him because He sees this as evidence that I
   don't trust Him and love Him as I should.
Because God loves me, He rejoices when I
   experience His power and strength and stand
   up under the pressure of life for His name's sake
Because God loves me, He keeps working
   patiently with me even when I feel like giving up
   and can't see why He doesn't give up with me
   too.

Because God loves me, He keeps on trusting
  me when at times I don't even trust myself.
Because God loves me, He never says there is
  no hope for me, rather, He patiently works
  with me, loves me and disciplines me in such
  a way that it is hard for me to understand the
  depth of His concern for me.
Because God loves me, He never forsakes me
  even though many of my friends might.

As you become secure in God's love, you will discover that you need not surrender your self-worth to the opinions and judgments of others, not even those of your father. God is for you!

Notes

1. Archibald Hart, *15 Principles for Achieving Happiness* (Waco, TX: Word Books, 1988), p. 114, adapted.
2. Jan Congo, *Free to Be God's Woman* (Ventura, CA: Regal Books, 1985), p. 27. Used by permission.
3. Jordan and Margaret Paul, *If You Really Loved Me* (Minneapolis, MN: CompCare Publications, 1987), adapted from pp. 127-128.
4. William and Kristi Gaultiere, *Mistaken Identity* (Old Tappan, NJ: Fleming H. Revell, 1989), p. 95. Used by permission.
5. William Fezler and Eleanor S. Field, *The Good Girl Syndrome* (NY: MacMillan, 1985), adapted from pp. 82, 133-136, 245-249.
6. Robert S. McGee, *The Search for Significance* (Houston, TX: Rapha Publishing, 1987), adapted from pp. 84-85.
7. David Seamands, *Healing of Memories* (Wheaton, IL: Victor Books, 1985), p. 11.
8. Gaultiere, *Mistaken Identity*, p. 56. Used by permission.
9. Congo, *Free to Be God's Woman*, p. 95.
10. Hart, *15 Principles for Achieving Happiness*, adapted from pp. 110-111.
11. Congo, *Free to Be God's Woman*, adapted from p. 94.

ELEVEN

Letting Your Father Off the Hook

One of my favorite pastimes is fishing—anywhere, anytime, under any conditions. The purpose of fishing, naturally, is to catch fish. But sometimes I wonder who is actually getting caught—the fish or me. Late one afternoon I was sitting on a dock of a large lake fishing and enjoying the pleasant weather. Suddenly a large fish took my bait and ripped off countless yards of line plummeting to the lake bottom to sulk. I was using light-weight leader, so I couldn't exert much pressure and I had to play him cautiously. I knew I was in for a long, slow fight.

As I sat waiting him out, rain clouds moved across the sky casting their dark shadows on the lake. Soon it began to sprinkle, then it began to pour. Within minutes I was soaked to the skin and chilled to the bone. I was also very hungry because it was dinner time and I had skipped lunch. I was miserable. Most fishermen would pack up and leave under those conditions. But I wanted to catch that fish, so I stayed.

My fish was stronger than I anticipated and it wasn't budging. The longer I played with him, the wetter, colder and hungrier I got. Then it hit me: I hadn't caught the fish; the dumb fish had caught me and was holding me captive! What to do? I could keep waiting it out for who knows how long and eventually bring it in. I could tug sharply on the line and inflict more pain on the fish, hoping to make him feel as miserable as I felt. Or I could just break the line, letting the fish and me off the hook and releasing us both from captivity. That day the fish and I both returned to our homes with little more than a great story to tell!

That fishing experience reminds me of the situation in which many adult daughters find themselves with their fathers. As an adult, you live where you want, go where you want and do what you want. You are finally free from your father's control—or are you? You may still be hooked to your father by feelings of pain, resentment, guilt or regret from his impact on your life. No matter what you do or where you go, there is still a nagging, restrictive emotional line tied between you.

You have the same three choices in your situation that I had with my big fish. First, you can remain miserable by refusing to let go of your father's offenses, continuing to carry the pain and resentment and allowing the past to dictate your present. You are making this choice when you avoid dealing with unresolved issues between you and your father. Second, you can actively fight your father, and complain about your past and your father's responsibility for it. This will keep your wounds, and his, open, raw and oozing. Third, you can choose to accept the past and its impact on you, then take the steps necessary to break its hold on you. You are no more the helpless victim of your past than I was the helpless victim of that big fish. You can choose to change your relationship with your father.

Cut the Line and Move On

Almost everyone has heard of Oprah Winfrey, one of television's leading talk-show hostesses. She is outgoing, articulate, poised and very much in control, belying the fact that she came from a wretched childhood and adolescence. As a young child, Oprah was tossed back and forth between feuding parents. Frequently she was sent to a grandmother who often beat her. "When my grandmother used to whip my behind," Oprah says, "she'd say, 'I'm doing this because I love you!' And I'd want to say, 'If you loved me, you'd get that switch off my butt.' I still don't think that was love."

*Your painful past relationship
with your father has caused you to
grow up believing certain things
about yourself, your father and
your relationship with him that
aren't true.*

When Oprah was nine she was raped by a 19-year-old cousin and lived in fear that she was pregnant. With these and other painful memories from her early years, Oprah Winfrey had good reason to be bitter and angry. Being hooked to her past could have ruined her present life, but she chose to overcome her past. "I understand that many people are victimized," she says, "and some people certainly more horribly than I have been. But you have to be responsible for claiming your own victories, you really do.

If you live in the past and allow the past to define who you are, then you never grow."[1]

If you do not cut the line to your past by dealing with the lingering residue of your father-daughter relationship, you will pay a steep price. Your price can include:

• feeling upset or angry after any contact with your father;
• living in anxiety-filled anticipation of any get-togethers with him;
• feeling guilty and struggling with shame;
• overreacting to men who remind you of your father;
• being controlled now and in the future by your past relationship;
• living with the effects of bitterness and alienation: an emotional drain.

If you compare this "price list" with the benefits of peace and freedom you receive from dealing with the past and moving on in your life, you will easily see which is the healthy choice. But when you decide to cut the line and move on, where do you begin? The rest of the chapter and the following chapter contain several suggestions which will help you let go of your past and grow into the future.

Identify the Problem

The first step in releasing the past is to become aware of the problems which still exist. Identify what it is from your past that still bothers you, affects you, influences you or hinders you. Take time to reflect on these issues and list them on paper. Then select one issue you would like to change. It could be a feeling of bitterness, hurt or rejection which has lingered from the past. It could be the hurtful way you and your father interact in person or on the phone. It could be feelings you have about yourself which stem from your past or present relationship with your father. It could be your damaging negative beliefs about yourself. Take whatever steps are necessary to clearly identify the problems involving your father and decide which of them will be the first one you will work toward eliminating. Take the same approach with subsequent issues, isolating them and dealing with them one by one.

It will also be helpful for you to identify the reasons why you want to work through these issues and change their impact on your life. Thoughtfully list these reasons below:

I want to change because . . .

1.
2.
3.
4.
5.
6
7.
8.
9.
10.

For some of you, the intensity of the trauma and hurt may have caused you to deny or suppress some of your memories of the incidents between you and your father. This sometimes occurs because you don't want to admit the severity of what happened to you. But when you repress and block out painful experiences and feelings, you often block out the good experiences also. As one woman told me, "It's as though I have selective amnesia. I know I existed during those years from four to ten, but my memory apparently went on vacation during that time to get away from the pain. I just can't remember anything from those years—good or bad."

How sad! Unfortunately, this woman's experience is fairly common. Wouldn't it be wonderful to recapture the good memories from those forgotten years! It *is* possible.

Some cases of memory gap indicate the possibility of traumatic abuse. Professional counseling and group support are very important to the healing process for these daughters. For the victims of childhood sexual abuse, I recommend the book, *The Right to Innocence: Healing the Trauma of Childhood Sexual Abuse* (Jeremy P. Tarcher, Inc.), by Beverly Engel.

Expose Your False Hidden Beliefs

The second step in cutting the line to your past is to identify and expose false hidden beliefs. Your painful past relationship with your father has caused you to grow up believing certain things about yourself, your father and your relationship with him that aren't true. For example, you may falsely believe that all men are abusive because your father was. Your belief is hidden in the sense that outwardly you admit that all men are not like your father, but subconsciously you withdraw from other men as if they are going to harm you.

Some of the beliefs you carry today have been blown way out of proportion; they're irrational. For example, the false belief that all men are abusive prevents some women from dating or befriending any men. These false beliefs must be exposed and corrected before you can move on in your life.

Your hidden beliefs are like invisible reins attached to you and held by your father. Many of the decisions in your life were probably made in response to the way he directly or indirectly pulled on the reins to direct you. Today you either move toward or away from people or events because of what you learned from the experiences of the past.

In order to uncover some of your false beliefs, answer the following questions regarding each issue or problem from your past you work through:

> As you were growing up, what did you decide was the best way to protect yourself and avoid future hurts in similar situations?
>
> What did you believe you must stop doing or give up in order to keep yourself from being hurt?
>
> What did you believe you had to become or do in order to feel secure and protected? Were these beliefs tied into gaining the love and acceptance of your father?
>
> What types of fears or concerns did you develop about other people and situations which were tied into your relationship with your father?[2]

Some women have discovered that they made self-limiting decisions based on false beliefs which caused them to be clinging, possessive or overcautious in their relationships, to avoid risks at all costs, to second-guess themselves, to not trust themselves, or to see their fathers in other men. An important question you must answer is, "What self-limiting decision did I make years ago which may have affected my life to the present?"[3]

You may falsely believe that what transpired between you and your father was so devastating and painful that you will be hindered by it for the rest of your life. You may have been emotionally rejected for years or physically or sexually abused. You may feel that the future is as bleak as your past. But that belief is false. There *is* hope. Recovery *is* possible. Change in feelings, attitudes and beliefs *can* occur. In cases where wounds from the past are deep and severe, it may take two or three years to work through the issues. In others where the hurt is not as severe, healing can occur in a much shorter amount of time.

Release Your Past

The third step to cutting the line is to let yourself and your father off the hook by releasing your past. In order to take this step you must believe that it is possible to leave past hurts behind. You can't use half-hearted phrases like, "Well, I'll try" or "I'll do it if . . . " You must make a determined commitment to change and move forward confidently on that commitment. Take charge of your life and your relationship with your father.

As you think about taking this step, your mind may be flooded with a number of objections. These thoughts usually come from a sense of powerlessness to change your situation. You may hear yourself complaining:

> I've had these feelings for such a long time. I can't change them.
>
> I'll always be this way.
>
> I've tried all that I know to do, but nothing works with my dad.
>
> I've never felt that Dad and I connected in the first place. Why should I try to change the relationship now?
>
> It's been this way for 35 years. I don't think I can

learn to handle the way he is. I'd rather avoid him.

I've tried for so long. I'm tired. It's not worth the effort.

Counteract these objections by committing yourself to practice consistently the suggestions in this chapter and the next for six months. Then you can decide if your inner statements are true or not. Give yourself a trial period for applying some new approaches to your relationship. Remember: You can change your attitudes, beliefs, responses and feelings whether or not your father changes.

If you are hesitant to move forward because you feel overwhelmed by the power your father has over you, remember: you gave him that power in the first place.

"That's an unfair statement," you may say. "I didn't give him power over me; he took it." Not really. If you have spent several years of your adult life allowing him to control you and your relationship, you *gave* him some of that power. If your father overpowered you as a child, that was his problem. But if he still overpowers you as an adult, that's your problem. He cannot overpower you now unless you give him that power. The more you give in to him now, the more you will reinforce his tendency to dominate you. You don't need to be dominated by him any longer. You can learn to respond to him more assertively and to gain freedom from his power over you.

Making changes in your relationship with your father and breaking loose from the past is similar to the experience of the Jews leaving Egypt to migrate to the Promised Land. When it came time to leave, they all wanted to go. But they soon discovered that the trip wasn't going to be easy. The Egyptian army came after them and they had to face the Red Sea and the desert. Many of the Jews wanted to return to Egypt because they feared the costs and risks of freedom more than they feared slavery. Leonard Felder describes the analogy this way:

> From a psychological point of view, this story of holding back just at the edge of freedom is a powerful metaphor of what goes on in our own lives. If you or I were in the desert with almost no water and the Egyptian soldiers were closing in, would we have stepped into the Red Sea and hoped we didn't drown? Surely, the enslavement we had known for years was awful, but at the same time it was familiar, predictable, orderly. On the other hand, freedom was an unknown, risky, unfamiliar, no guarantees, it might not last. Needless to say, arguments broke out and many wanted to turn back. Most people are more comfortable holding onto their emotional enslavements than risking something new and uncertain.[4]

Breaking free from the past involves a process of recovery. What is recovery? It is being able to reflect upon your past and how it contributed to your identity, both positive and negative, without allowing the negative to control your present life. Recovery is finding new meaning to your present life by ridding yourself of the contamination of the past. It means claiming your circumstances instead of letting your circumstances claim your happiness.[5]

Plotting Your Past

A helpful tool for releasing your past is the Father Relationship History Graph. The purpose of the graph is to help you identify significant events in your past involving your father which impacted your life, both positively and negatively. Here's a sample graph:

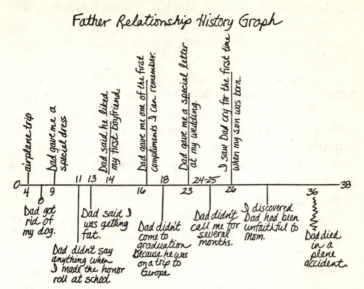

Father Relationship History Graph

At this point, put the book down and create your own Father Relationship History Graph. Draw a horizontal line in the middle of a blank sheet of paper. The line represents your life from birth, on the left end, to the present, on the right end. Indicate your father's impact on your life by describing specific events along the time line, noting your age when they happened. Write your positive experiences with your father above the time line and your negative experiences below the time line.

The length of the line you draw from the time line to your description of the event represents how intensely the experience influenced you. The longer the line, the greater the intensity. A straight line indicates that the event no longer influences you and a wavy line indicates that the event still influences you today.

After you complete your graph, it will be helpful for you to share it with another person. You may feel comfortable talking with a woman who has created her own graph. Or you may find it beneficial to ask your husband to graph his experiences with his father, then discuss your graphs together.

As you study your graph, are there more positive experiences than negative experiences? As you think about your positive experiences, which ones have you discussed with your father? Is he aware that you regard these experiences as a positive influence on your life? If not, how would you describe these experiences to him? How would you like him to respond if you told him about these positive experiences?

As you consider the negative experiences on your graph, answer the following questions:

Which ones have been difficult for you to acknowledge that they occurred?

Which ones have you and your father never discussed or settled?

If you discussed these experiences with a friend or spouse, did any of them elicit an emotional response from you (tightness in the throat, tears, etc.)? If so, what triggered the response?

Which of these experiences would you like to discuss with your father?

What do you hope to accomplish by sharing them with him?

How do you hope he will respond?

How might you be different if you share these experiences with him?

How will you handle it if he does not respond positively when you share with him? Can you share your feelings with him for your own benefit and be satisfied regardless of his response?

Do you need to forgive your father for any of these experiences?

Is there any information about your father that you need to discover which will help you understand him and his actions better? If so, how will you discover it?

What are you hesitant to ask or to share with your father? Why?

Confronting your father is the final step in the process of releasing him and yourself from the pains of your past. If you choose to use the graph as the basis for your confrontation, complete the following steps in preparation for your meeting:

1. Write a paragraph (or several if necessary) describing each incident on your graph, including the feelings you experienced when it occurred and your feelings now. Indicate how that event is still affecting your life at the present time.

2. For each event, write exactly what you want to say to your father if you discuss it with him.

3. If you don't or can't discuss these events with him, describe in writing how you will break free from each incident's hold on you.

4. Describe how you will relinquish your feelings about each event if you don't or can't confront your father.

5. If you plan to confront your father on these incidents, write four or five of his typical responses you expect to hear from him. For each of these responses, write how you will respond. Practice your responses aloud, on

tape or with a friend who can coach you as you learn to respond to your father in a new manner.[6]

If that sounds like a lot of work to you, you're right. But you will find the results of your preparation to be well worth the effort.

Confrontation: Bringing Down the Curtain

The final step to unhooking yourself from your painful past relationship with your father is a confrontation with him. Although you can experience a large measure of healing from the past by completing the previous steps, confrontation is often the necessary final act which will bring down the curtain on your past.

Confrontation is simply and essentially a sharing of facts and feelings. It is not a vindictive attack or an argument. It is not intended to alienate or change anyone. You do not confront someone for the purpose of releasing your anger against them. In fact, it is best to release your anger before a confrontation. You do not confront someone to punish him, get even with him, frighten him or make him suffer.

Rather, confrontation is a way of bringing closure to a painful relationship from the past that would continue to fester if it was not openly discussed and dealt with. For the believer in Jesus Christ, confrontation is also a step in appropriating God's forgiveness for yourself and for the person you are confronting. Confrontation is an act of love, especially for those with whom your relationship is going to continue. And even for those you are not close to, confrontation is a loving way to inform them of their impact on you so they can take responsibility for their actions. Confrontation will be a growing experience for those you confront and it will free you for healthier confrontations with others in your life.[7]

For those who were severely victimized in their younger years, confrontation serves an additional purpose. Standing up to your past will help you prove to yourself that you will not be victimized or dominated by that person again, nor will you live in fear of him.

Confrontation is a practical application of the instruction in the Word of God telling us to speak the truth in love (Eph. 4:15). You must confront your father truthfully by telling him exactly how you feel about the past. Proverbs 28:23 reads, "In the end, people appreciate frankness more than flattery" (*TLB*). But your frank confrontation must be done in love in order to heal your relationship, not damage it further.

When it comes to deciding on a method for confrontation, you have two major choices: indirect or direct confrontation. In indirect confrontation, you are confronting your problems and feelings *without* actually confronting your father. An indirect confrontation may involve writing a letter to your father which you read aloud to an empty chair, a friend or a tape recorder, but do not send to your father. This approach allows you the security of keeping your encounter private and distant. You can also say what you want to say without interruption and not get personally involved with your father's response. The disadvantage of the indirect method is that you will never know the sense of completion which comes from sharing face-to-face and receiving a firsthand response.

If you opt for a direct confrontation, you have some additional choices to consider, namely a letter, a phone call or a face-to-face visit. If you choose to send a letter, be sure to write and refine several drafts. Read it aloud to see how it sounds. Some women have found it helpful to read it to someone else for an objective evaluation. I have read several of them.

Confronting through a letter eliminates the possibility of freezing or becoming tongue-tied in a face-to-face confrontation. Also, if your father is visually-oriented, a letter to read may penetrate him deeper than a face-to-face conversation. The disadvantage of this method is the large possibility that your father may not respond to your letter. You may suffer from not knowing if he read it, understood it or accepted it.

If you are still being abused by your father in any way—emotionally, verbally, sexually or physically—you must confront him in person.

If you prefer to confront your father by telephone, prepare what you want to say in advance. You may even want to work from a set of notes to guide your interaction with him. The disadvantage of this method is missing out on over half of your father's response because you cannot see his nonverbal expressions. Also, your father could put the phone down and not listen to you, or literally hang up on you during your message.

A face-to-face confrontation eliminates the disadvantage of receiving a partial or total nonresponse. By confronting your father in person, you can make sure that he hears and understands what you have to say. And you will be able to see and hear his reactions. Meeting him in person also conveys the importance of your message. Many fathers are quite receptive in face-to-face confrontations.

Some are totally amazed at what they hear. They are unaware that what they did—or did not do—impacted their daughters so forcefully. I know fathers who have apologized to their daughters after a confrontation, leading to a very meaningful time of forgiveness and healing.

A face-to-face confrontation can be pressure-filled, however, because you have no control over your father's response. He may interrupt you defensively or lash out angrily. You may end up feeling trapped in the situation and wishing you had selected a less direct approach.

When is a face-to-face confrontation necessary? If you are still being abused by your father in any way—emotionally, verbally, sexually or physically—you must confront him in person. If you are still so deeply controlled by your father that you cannot be an individual in your own right, you must confront him in person. If you live in fear of your father, you need to face that fear with a personal confrontation. And if you are concerned that your father may be abusing your children in some way, you must deal with him face-to-face.[8]

Preparation and practice are essential to the success of a face-to-face confrontation. First of all, spend time praying for yourself and your father. Ask the Lord to help you recall and identify the past hurts which are directing your present life. Above all, pray for the Lord's timing. Don't rush into a direct confrontation. Wait awhile. Some daughters have waited months, even years, before the time was right to confront their fathers. Allow the Holy Spirit to lead you.

Next, make a list of the hurts and how they have affected you. Your list may include how your father slighted you, disappointed you, disapproved of you, deserted you, rejected you, berated you or abused you emotionally, sexually or physically. Then list all the feelings which resulted from his actions, such as fear, anger, shame, worthlessness, guilt, inner pain, etc. Indicate the effects you personally experienced as a child, adolescent and adult, and the effects which presently impact your own family, husband and children.

Then write down exactly what you want to say to your father and the way you need to say it in order to be heard by him. Be sure your statements begin with "I feel" or "I want" instead of accusatory words like "You never" or "You should have." List everything you wanted from him when you were younger that you didn't receive. Be specific. Finally, indicate what you want from him now. Again, be specific.

Here are examples from two women who listed their specific disappointments and wants. The first woman was disappointed and rejected by her father, and the second woman was a victim of sexual abuse:

In the past . . .

I wanted you to tell me that I was pretty.
I wanted you to take time to play with me.
I wanted you to encourage me.
I wanted you to listen to me.
I wanted you to share with me who you really were.

In the present . . .

I want you to be more involved in my life and our family.
I want you to ask me questions and then listen to me.

I want you to call me once a week and spend several minutes sharing what's going on in your life.

I want my children to get to know you. Please spend time with them.

In the past . . .

I wanted you to stop touching me in the wrong places.

I wanted you to tell me I was all right and that you were at fault.

I wanted you to go away and leave me and my sister alone.

In the present . . .

I want you to know how you affected my life.

I want you to admit what you did and seek the counseling you never received.

I want you to get well and be who you were supposed to be.

I want to know you can be trusted.

Practice your confrontation by delivering your message aloud, perhaps on tape so you can listen to yourself and make improvements. Consider role-playing the confrontation with a trusted friend playing the role of your father.

Decide when and where you will talk with your father. Meeting him in his own territory may put you at a disadvantage. You may want to select a neutral setting such as a restaurant or a park. Take confidence and strength from the Lord, knowing that He loves you and your father and wants to work in you both to affect a healthy relationship.

A major element which must undergird the entire process of releasing the past and confronting your father is forgiveness. You cannot be healed from your hurts nor can your relationship with your father be resolved unless you forgive him and forgive yourself for what happened. The next chapter addresses the vital issue of forgiveness as it relates to your father-daughter relationship.

Notes

1. Kevin Leman and Randy Carlson, *Unlocking the Secrets of Childhood Memories* (Nashville, TN: Thomas Nelson Publishers, 1989), adapted from pp. 137-138.
2. Leonard Felder, *A Fresh Start* (NY: Signet Books, 1987), adapted from pp. 25-26.
3. Ibid.
4. Felder, *A Fresh Start*, p. 43. Used by permission.
5. John W. James and Frank Cherry, *The Grief Recovery Handbook* (San Francisco: Harper and Row, 1988), adapted from p. 7.
6. Ibid., adapted from pp. 105, 114-120.
7. Beverly Engel, *The Right to Innocence* (LA: Jeremy P. Tarcher, Inc., 1989), adapted from pp. 108-110.
8. Ibid., adapted from pp. 118-128.

TWELVE

Giving the Gift of Forgiveness

Victoria described her relationship with her father to me one day:

> My memories of my father are unpleasant and vague. He didn't seem that interested in me at any time when I was growing up. He was brusque and gruff. I always had to go to him to show him things; he never came to me. Even then he didn't say much. One of the things I hated most was his anger. He would shout and storm around, then not talk to any of us for several days. For some reason I always felt responsible for his outbursts. And Dad practically lived at work. It was like pulling teeth to get him to take a vacation.
>
> I guess I hoped for so much more from him: a word of praise here, a compliment there. He just grunted when I showed him my high school prom dress. When I call him now we talk a little, but it's

never anything more than surface level. I wish he would open up to me. He talks for awhile and then says, "Here's your mother."

As we continued to talk, I asked Victoria some questions about her father's background and upbringing. The more we discussed her father, the more she recalled about him. We were able to develop a profile of her father which included the following facts:

- He was raised in a home with his parents and three domineering brothers.
- His father was quiet and hard-working.
- He had little contact with girls as a young man.
- He didn't date until age 32 when he met and married Victoria's mother.
- He didn't relate well to or communicate much with anyone. He didn't have close friends.
- He wanted to make sure his family was financially secure because his parents struggled so to make a living.
- Much of the time he looked like he wanted to say something, but never could find the words.

After we discussed her father's upbringing and identified some of the reasons behind his failures as a father, Victoria began to see him in new light. She realized that he was a human being with faults and weaknesses, and she was able to accept his inability to provide what she needed as a girl. Victoria's deep-seated anger toward her father melted away in the warmth of her understanding and forgiveness. Forgiveness is an integral element in the entire process of coming to terms with your relationship with your father and releasing the past and its hurts.

Angry Daughters

One of the greatest obstacles to forgiveness is anger. Like Victoria, you may be angry at your father for his failures and mistakes in the past. If so, admit it and deal with it. Yes, it takes courage to admit your anger. But learning to release your anger in a healthy manner can affect your life in a positive way. You have a choice. Repressing or suppressing anger is like carrying a gun which is loaded and cocked. Eventually it will go off and somebody will get hurt. But releasing anger constructively defuses the ammunition and empties the gun.

Women who were severely traumatized by their fathers as children are often angry adult daughters. And many of them tend to direct their anger at themselves by taking the blame for what happened to them. Blaming yourself for what your father did is like turning that loaded gun on yourself. Don't accept misdirected anger or blame; throw it away! One therapist suggests closing your eyes and imagining that you are throwing all those feelings at the person to whom they belong. Then, while in a room alone, open your eyes and make a throwing motion with your arm while saying aloud, "Take this. It doesn't belong to me. It belongs to you."[1]

There are numerous benefits to constructively releasing your anger. Here are several of them:

Releasing your anger will . . .

- improve your self-esteem. When you stop blaming yourself, your self-esteem will grow stronger.
- give you hope. You will feel as if a tremendous burden has been lifted from your shoulders. It takes a huge amount of energy to hold down all that anger.

- release physical tension. When you start releasing your anger, your body will become more relaxed, more mobile.
- free you to express love and joy, and to experience feelings of pleasure.
- clarify your thinking and improve your decision-making abilities. Your thinking will become less confused when you are less distracted by your anger.
- empower you physically and emotionally, and help make you more assertive.
- help you become an independent person, enabling you to mentally and emotionally separate from your parents and leave destructive relationships.
- improve your relationships. You will be less likely to take your anger out on your mate, children, friends and co-workers.
- affirm your innocence.
- help you become a survivor instead of remaining a victim.

If accepting and releasing anger is difficult for you, identify why you are resisting it. Think about and complete the following statements, then share your answers with a trusted friend and ask him or her to confirm or expand on your ideas:

I am afraid to release my anger because . . .

I don't want to release my anger because . . . [2]

If you have difficulty releasing your anger, it may be because you are getting some faulty messages from others. For example, someone may say, "You shouldn't express your anger; it's not Christian. Besides, it isn't healthy to release your anger. Why release your anger when you can simply forgive?" Forgiveness is important, but it's the final step in a series of progressive steps which begins with dealing with anger. I like the suggestions Beverly Engel gives as possible responses to those who say you shouldn't release your anger:

The past is *not* past; it is still here ruining my life.

I'm not trying to change the past, I'm changing the way I'm dealing with it.

I'm angry because I was hurt. I can't work on forgiving until I release my anger.

I have a right to be angry. If you want to help me, you will try to encourage me to release it.[3]

How to Release Anger

There are several important steps to constructively releasing the anger you hold toward your father. The first four steps are a series which should be followed in sequence. Steps 5 and 6 are additional steps you should plan on including in your personal exercise of releasing anger.

1. Identify your feelings. List on paper all the resentments, hurts and angry feelings you hold toward your father. Describe in writing exactly what happened to you in as much detail as possible, and how you felt about it then and how you feel now. Here are some examples women have shared with me:

I feel hurt that you made sarcastic remarks about my weight in front of others. I feel angry that you didn't ever give me approval. I feel there's something wrong with me. I resent that you wouldn't listen to me.

I resent the fact that you ran around on Mother and made me carry that secret as well.

I feel angry for the way you try to use me for your own benefit. I feel cheap.

I resent your not loving me for who I am.

I'm angry that my life is so messed up today because I wanted to prove to you that I'm "no darn good," just like you said I was.

I resent you and all men.

I'm angry that you've never communicated with me. Who in the world are you?

Please be aware that you may experience considerable emotional upheaval as you make your list. Other old, previously buried feelings may surface at this time and you may feel upset for awhile. As you think about and work on this list, ask God to reveal to you the deep, hidden pools of painful memories so your inner container of anger may be emptied. Thank Him that it is all right for you to wade through and expel these feelings at this time. Imagine Jesus Christ in the room with you saying, "I want you to be cleansed and free. You don't have to be emotionally lame, blind or deaf any longer because of what happened to you."

Don't show your list to anyone and don't give it to your father. Releasing your anger at this point is not a face-to-face confrontation.

Imagine Jesus Christ in the room with you saying, "I want you to be cleansed and free. You don't have to be emotionally lame, blind or deaf any longer because of what happened to you."

---

2. Set your list aside. After writing as many feelings as possible, set your list aside and rest for awhile. Allow a period of time to recall other feelings you need to share which did not appear on your first list. Add these to your list as you remember them. You probably will not remember all your hurts, but you don't need to for this exercise to succeed.

3. Read your list aloud. Take your list into a room where there are two empty chairs facing each other. Sit in one of the chairs and imagine your father sitting in the other. See your father welcoming you in a positive manner. Hear him saying something like, "I want to hear what you have to share with me. I will accept it. Please tell me what's on your heart. I need to hear it."

Look at the empty chair as though your father was there. Take your time reading your list aloud to your imagined father. At first you may feel awkward or embarrassed about reading aloud in an empty room. But these feelings will pass. You may even find yourself amplifying what you have written as you share your list. Feel free to do so.

As you share, imagine that your father is listening to you, nodding in acceptance and understanding your feelings. You may experience intense anger, depression, anxiety or other feelings as you continue with your list. Share these feelings with your imaginary father also. Remember: Not only is he giving you permission to share your past and present feelings, but Jesus Christ is there also, giving you permission to release your anger.

You may find that talking through only one of the feelings on your list is all you can handle at this time. If you find yourself becoming emotionally drained, it is important to stop and rest for awhile. After some time of relaxation, resume your normal tasks for the day. Continue working through your list of feelings at another time.

4. Let Jesus heal you. Before you conclude your time of sharing, close your eyes and visualize yourself, your father and Jesus standing together with your hands on each other's shoulders. Spend several minutes visualizing this scene. At this point you may want to imagine that your father does not accept what you have said to him. This may be closer to reality than what you imagined earlier. But see yourself at peace regardless.

Once you have completed these four steps, you may find that you need to repeat them several times over a period of weeks until the hurts of your past are no more than a memory.

5. Write a letter. Another helpful method for releasing your anger is to write a letter to your father—a letter you will not send him. This exercise is for your benefit, to help you verbalize your feelings.

Begin your letter as you would any letter to him: "Dear Dad." Don't worry about style, neatness or proper grammar and punctuation. You are simply identifying, expressing and releasing your feelings toward him. It may be difficult getting started, but as you begin to write you will find your words and feelings flowing out. Don't hold back! Let out all the feelings of anger, hurt and resentment which have been churning inside you. Don't evaluate at this time whether your feelings are good or bad, right or wrong. They exist and they need to be expressed. This exercise will probably leave you emotionally drained. Plan on allowing yourself some time to rest.

Sometimes I have clients in therapy write such a letter at home and bring it to their next session. Often a client will try to hand her letter to me as she walks in the office. I refuse to take it. I tell her, "I'd like you to keep the letter and we will use it in a little while." At the appropriate time, I ask her to imagine that her father is sitting in an empty chair in the office. Then I have her read the letter aloud as if her father was listening.

It will be helpful for you to share your letter in a similar way in the hearing of your husband or another close relative, or a trusted friend. It should be someone who will listen and be supportive, and who will not make value judgments on you or your letter or violate your confidence. Sit across from your friend and read the letter aloud. Invite your friend to make comments, but only those that support you in what you are sharing and encourage you to share more. The experience of sharing your letter in the presence of a caring person can implement your healing. Be sure to thank him or her for listening.

6. Project a positive response. There is one more step which is a very important part of the healing process.

After you release your negative emotions of anger and resentment, it is essential that you project a positive response such as love, acceptance or friendship toward your father. If you do not replace the negative feelings with a positive response, you become emotionally neutral toward your father. You become blasé—no feelings toward him at all. I've had a number of clients tell me that they feel nothing toward their fathers. They have developed a state of emotional insulation, which means they have blocked off the expression of all feelings, and that's not healthy. Having released your anger and resentment, you must immediately begin responding toward your father in a positive way.

Forgiving Your Father

If you find yourself resisting the expression of positive emotions toward your father, there may be some vestiges of unresolved resentment still hiding within you. This next exercise is a means of uncovering those feelings and clearing the way for your positive response.

Take a blank sheet of paper and write the salutation at the top, "Dear Dad." Under the salutation, write the words "I forgive you for . . . " Then complete the sentence by stating something your father did which has bothered you all these years. For example, a daughter may write, "I forgive you for always trying to control my life."

Next, capture the first thought that comes to mind after writing your sentence. It may be a thought which contradicts the concept of forgiveness you are trying to express. It may be an emotional rebuttal or protest to what you have just written. For example, the woman who is forgiving her father for controlling her life may remember how he forbade her from dating a boy she liked because his father was a blue collar worker, not a professional like her father. Her thought ignites an area of resentment which was smoldering within her.

Whatever the thought is, write another "I forgive you for . . . " statement for it. The daughter with a controlling father may write, "I forgive you for forbidding me to date the boy I liked." Keep writing "I forgive you for . . . " statements for every thought or feeling that comes to the surface. Don't be discouraged if your angry protests contradict the concept of forgiveness or are so firm and vehement that it seems like you have not expressed any forgiveness at all. You are in the process of forgiving your father, so keep writing until all the pockets of resentment and resistance have been drained.

Some people finish this exercise with only a few statements. Others have a great deal of resentment to clear away and they continue writing for several pages. You will know you have emptied your inner container of resentment when you write "I forgive you for . . . " and can think of no more resentful responses to complete the statement.

After you have completed writing, sit facing an empty chair and read aloud your list of statements of forgiveness. Visualize your father sitting there accepting your forgiveness with both verbal and nonverbal affirmation. Take as long as you need for this step, explaining and amplifying your statements as you go if necessary.

It is important that you show this list to no one. When you are finished verbalizing your statements, destroy the entire list. Burn it or tear it into little pieces symbolizing that "the old has gone, the new has come!" (2 Cor. 5:17).

Forgiveness involves letting go. Remember playing tug-of-war as a child? As long as the parties on each end of

the rope are tugging, you have a "war." But when someone lets go, the war is over. When you forgive your father,
you are letting go of your end of the rope. No matter how
hard he may tug on the other end, if you have released
your end, the war is over for you.

Letting go isn't always easy, as Dwight Wolter
explains:

> Letting go is a difficult thing to do. The dynamics of a
> dysfunctional home keep us plugged in and holding on
> for dear life. Many of us have been trying for years to
> make a bad situation feel right. When someone even
> mentions the possibility of letting go, we begin to feel
> as if we are being asked to relax and prepare for take-
> off when the cockpit door is open and we can see that
> a child is in the driver's seat of the plane. We have to
> learn to take the child out of the driver's seat and
> trust that our adult self is capable of getting us where
> we want to go. Letting go is an integral part of for-
> giveness. We can begin by being willing to let go of
> our unforgiving stance. We can admit that the events
> and feelings of our childhood really happened. We can
> stop blaming ourselves for what is essentially a family
> problem . . . . We can admit to ourselves that, try as
> we may, the past cannot be undone. We can let go of
> our hope for a better yesterday.[4]

At one time in your life you may have accepted that
your father knew what he was doing. You believed that he
knew what was right and wrong, and he always did what
was right. Perhaps most of the time he did; but perhaps
not. Like Victoria at the beginning of this chapter, you
need to see your father as a man with weaknesses, a man
who made mistakes. Your father had his own difficult back-

ground and personal deficits, and these have probably impacted you. At some point you need to accept the reality of who your father was and is. Then, without excusing his behavior, you need to let go of those negative experiences by forgiving him. It's the only method of ending the war between you that you have control over.

Forgiving Yourself

Along with forgiving your father for his negative impact on your life, you need to forgive yourself. Why forgive yourself? There are numerous reasons. You may be blaming yourself and feeling guilty for:

- not being able to change—or cure—your father;
- not living up to his spoken expectations for you;
- not being loved and accepted by him, which you attributed to a defect in your appearance or personality;
- not being perfect in some way or every way;
- treating yourself the way your father treated you;
- mistreating yourself when you have difficult times;
- choosing men like your father in hopes that you can reform them;
- developing some of the same tendencies or problems you despise in your father.

We often take out our frustrations, not on the person who hurt us, but on ourselves. We do this because we subconsciously consider ourselves a safer target than the person we are struggling with. After all, your father has hurt you in the past. You feel that you can't vent your frustrations on him because he will only hurt you again. So you take the path of least resistance by shouldering the blame yourself. Again, blaming yourself is like playing with a loaded gun. You will eventually get hurt. You must release self-blame by forgiving yourself.

When you fail to forgive yourself, you may also take out your feelings on anyone who happens to get in your way. Unfortunately, the innocent bystanders often happen to be your husband and children. When you see the same defects in them that you see in yourself, you react to them, usually in an unhealthy way. Your children do not have the resources to handle your guilt-driven responses of silence, anger, rejection or abuse. So for their sake also, you need to forgive yourself.

Much of the guilt and blame you feel may be tied to your behavior as a child in response to your father's influence. Be aware that you were not responsible for what happened to you as a young child. You didn't have either the coping mechanisms or the defenses to make the right responses. You can see this today in the way a child handles a crisis. In a moment of fear, a six-year-old may revert to behaving like a three-year-old because that's the only way she knows how to respond to fear. She's not at fault for responding like a three-year-old. She just hasn't accumulated the life experiences to develop a repertoire of appropriate responses. Forgive yourself for the way you handled your father when you were a child. You are not to blame.

You may also need to forgive yourself for adult behaviors you *are* responsible for in your relationship with your father. Let me remind you of an important passage from the Word of God: "If we walk in the light as He Himself is in the light, we have fellowship with one another, and the blood of Jesus His Son cleanses us from all sin . . . . If we confess our sins, He is faithful and righteous to forgive us our sins and to cleanse us from all unrighteousness" (1

John 1:7,9, *NASB*). If God has forgiven your sins, who are you to contradict Him? Take God's perspective on your failures and forgive yourself.

In order to help you discover areas where you need to forgive yourself, complete the following exercise on a separate sheet of paper:

Your life as a child:

1. List some of the bad things you did because of your relationship with your father.
2. For each behavior, list at least two reasons why you think you did it.
3. For which of these behaviors do you feel personally responsible?
4. Complete this statement: I feel I need to forgive myself for . . .
5. Complete this statement: I accept the forgiveness of Jesus Christ for the following things I did as a child:

Your life as an adult:

1. What have you done as an adult which is a direct result of your relationship with your father?
2. For each behavior, list at least two reasons why you think you did it.
3. For which of these behaviors do you feel personally responsible?
4. Complete this statement: I feel I need to forgive myself for . . .
5. Complete this statement: I accept the forgiveness of Jesus Christ for the following things I did as an adult . . . .

Perhaps it would be helpful if you wrote yourself a letter of forgiveness and then read it to yourself. Consider basing your letter on the statements of forgiveness found in God's Word. He wants us to be forgiven people.

Forgive and Move Ahead

One of the delights of counseling is to witness the reconciliation of a father and his adult daughter. I have seen an emotionally distant adult daughter develop a caring relationship with her aged father. I have seen an abused daughter develop a healthy relationship with her father through the forgiveness which Jesus Christ allows us to experience. For some of you, when you forgive your father, you will move into a closer relationship with him. For others, you will forgive your father, but you will still be distant from him because he chooses not to change. But remember: When you acknowledge and release your anger, and forgive your father for anything and everything he has done, you have let go of your end of the rope and the war is over.

The only way to be free, to move ahead in life and to experience God's abundance and grace is through the release of forgiveness.

The only way to be free, to move ahead in life and to experience God's abundance and grace is through the release of forgiveness. In order to finalize your act of forgiveness, write a statement of release which fits your situation with your father. Here are some statements of release you can use as models for your statement:

> Dad, I release you from the responsibility I have given you to determine how I feel and how I respond to others in my life. I release you from the bitterness and resentment which I have held toward you and others in my life because of you. This includes bitterness over . . .

> I release you from being responsible for my happiness. I release you from my expectations of who you should have been, what you should have done and . . .
> I forgive you.

Finally, if your father is still living, spend time praying for him. Pray about his weaknesses, pray for his growth and ask God's blessing upon his life. Release your past and your father to the Lord. Pray about the new freedom in your relationship that you are in the process of discovering. Pray for the Lord's renewing strength and ask Him to incorporate into your life His view of you as forgiven and free.

Notes

1. Beverly Engel, *The Right to Innocence* (LA: Jeremy P. Tarcher, Inc., 1989), p. 92.
2. Ibid., p. 98. Used by permission.
3. Ibid., p. 105. Used by permission.
4. Dwight Lee Wolter, *Forgiving Our Parents* (Minneapolis, MN: CompCare Publishers, 1989), adapted from pp. 55-56.

THIRTEEN

Releasing Your Father

Recently I came across Margaret's story, which graphically illustrates what many of us have experienced or will experience:

> When I went home for Christmas last December, I knew something was wrong the minute Dad came to greet me in the driveway. Usually a powerfully built and vital man, he'd lost weight, his face was thin and pale, and his eyes looked glassy. "What's wrong?" I asked. "Nothing," he insisted. It wasn't until after we had all spent Christmas Day together that Dad went to bed early and Mom broke the news to me. Dad had a tumor. He was going in for tests to see whether "it" had spread. I asked Mom if "it" meant cancer. She looked away as though she believed that if no one used the word "cancer" the problem might go away.
>
> The next day I kept thinking, "This couldn't have

come at a worse time in my career," for I had just been promoted to assistant producer—the first time a woman had held that position on our show. I wasn't ready for Dad's illness and all it entailed. When Mom called me with the test results, I was in shock. "It can't be true," I thought. Why was Dad so stubborn all those years when we tried unsuccessfully to get him to stop smoking? Crazily, I even resented my best friend, Vickie, whose father had recently gone in for tests and found out that the lump on his prostate was benign.

Dad's cancer was so widespread the doctors advised against surgery. Offering only some unproven experimental drugs, they said he had just a few months to live. While I hated the idea of my father being used as a guinea pig, Mom insisted, "Your father and I have talked it over with the doctors, and we feel that if there's a chance they can keep him alive, it's worth the price."

Since the drugs were making him vomit and lose his hair, I spent the next several days running up hundreds of dollars in phone bills searching for an alternative therapy Dad would agree to. Every time I broached the subject with Mom, she became furious. The doctors accused me of trying to get in the way of my father's treatments. My father was angry that I would even consider challenging his faith in the doctors.

In his dreary hospital room, Dad spent most of his time asleep or in a drugged state. The few times he felt like talking were no better. His condition made him impatient and short-tempered; nearly every night he'd ask me questions like why I wasn't marrying a nice Catholic professional instead of dating my

Jewish screenwriter friend. I tried to conceal my hurt feelings, but no matter what I said, it was the wrong thing. Each time I kissed my father's forehead I couldn't help thinking this might be the last time. Part of me wanted the ordeal to be over and for him to die, while deep inside I could feel myself desperately crying, "Daddy, don't leave me."[1]

Margaret's cry is the cry many of us will utter, or have already uttered, at the death of our fathers. Fathers become ill, grow old and die. This is reality. But the inevitability of your father's aging and death doesn't make it any easier to deal with. As you observe the process happening, you may experience feelings of anxiety and discomfort you've never felt before. The grieving process often begins long before father departs. If you have a deep, loving relationship with your father, you grieve over what you will eventually lose. If your relationship is lacking in love and depth, you grieve over what you never had.

It's difficult for some women to think of their fathers getting old. "That's something that happens to other men, not my father," one woman told me. She was struggling with the need to place her father in a care center since she could no longer care for him herself. You may also be struggling with your father's aging and the thought of his death. You may be frustrated at his changing behavior, perhaps feeling that much of his negative behavior is directed at you. Understanding your father's aging process will better help you prepare to release him when he dies.

Signs of the Times

Several telltale signs may accompany your father's aging process. He may slow down in his thinking and his physical movement and reflexes. His ability to cope with things he used to handle well begins to wane. The older he grows, the more he moves into the realm of helplessness. This feeling is very threatening to many men because it implies a loss of control. And for a man, control is where it's at!

You may begin to note some changes in your father when he retires. For many men, work contributes structure and a sense of worth to their lives. Retirement often strips those away. It is not unusual for men to become increasingly depressed and dependent at the end of their careers.

Many of your father's characteristics may intensify as he ages, especially his negative characteristics. If he has been withdrawn most of his life, he may withdraw even more. If he tended to play the role of the martyr, he is likely to play it to the hilt and find new ways of evoking guilt in you and other family members. If he was a tyrant, he may get even more harsh and domineering. You hope that he will mellow with age in a positive direction. But as his arteries harden and brain function diminishes, some of your father's behaviors may become unreasonable and he may be incapable of change.

As you and your parents age, role reversal gradually occurs. The parent becomes the child and the child becomes the parent. Your parents may even revert to childish behavior. Over a period of years control and responsibility shifts from your parents' shoulders to you. It's your turn to take care of them. Dr. Leopold Bellak describes the transition from parenting children to parenting parents:

> This is the moment, maybe even the very first opportunity, to relax a bit, to take a vacation unencumbered by diapers, childish squabbles, measles,

colds, or school calendar. But wait, what's this? Suddenly a new crop of "children" has been harvested. The middle-aged adults look around and notice that their parents, while not at present helpless, are approaching the age when they will need looking after.[2]

Taking responsibility for parenting your parents means becoming involved with them as they were involved with you when you were a child. If you have not already made statements like the following to your father, it probably won't be long before you do:

Dad, are you sick? Have you told Mom how badly you feel? Have you called the doctor? Yes, you have the doctor's phone number in your book. He's been your doctor for many years. Do you want me to call him and see about getting you in? Do you want me to take you to his office?

Hello, Dad. I just called to see if you took your medicine today. I know it tastes bad, but it's good for you and the doctor says you must take it.

Dad, you shouldn't walk to the post office without your coat. It's too cold for you to be outside in the mornings without a coat on.

Here, Dad, give me the hedge trimmer. You're not handling it too well and I don't want you to hurt yourself.

Sometimes the transition is difficult for both father and adult daughter. Mary came to my office one day trying to figure out what to do about her father. "He's so stubborn," she said. "He knows what he can and can't do, yet he persists in trying things that he can no longer do and he makes a mess. Frankly, I'm getting tired of him not listening to me when I know what's best for him."

When you tell your father what he can't do, he will either try to prove to you and to himself that he can do it or he will wither and retreat in defeat.

But when a man has been strong, capable and independent, he doesn't want to give that up or admit his incapabilities. And you, as his child, must be careful not to take away his sense of freedom, hope, usefulness and worth. If you do, you may stifle his will to live, especially if he is a widower. The National Institute of Mental Health indicates that widowers are significantly more likely to die than other men at the same age who have not lost their wives. This increased risk persists for at least the first six years after his wife's death, unless the man remarries. There is also an increased risk of suicide among those who have lost their mates.[3]

When you tell your father what he can't do, he will either try to prove to you and to himself that he can do it or he will wither and retreat in defeat. As you move into the role of parenting him, you must do so as a helper. As difficult as it is, you must avoid being short-tempered, condescending, impatient and judgmental with him.

Dealing with Feelings and Decisions

You will experience a wide range of feelings as you watch your parents grow older, especially if they behave in some of the ways Dr. Bellak describes:

> Your mother may have become absent-minded; her mind wanders or she imagines she hears and sees things, or she complains about people being *after her*. Or your two elderly parents may have started quarreling with bitterness that exceeds anything you have ever heard before. One may accuse the other of infidelity. Mother may accuse father of trying to poison her; father may say she is always hiding his money. Perhaps they will tell you of the meanness of neighbors who keep them awake by moving furniture around in the middle of the night or by spying on them. Let me reassure you, complaints like these— bizarre as they may seem to you on first hearing— are rather frequent.[4]

When you see your father behaving so differently, you may become angry and impatient with him. Isn't that a strange reaction toward a loved one? Not really; it's quite normal. You may feel these emotions because you are straining to handle the burden of your father's increased limitations or because his behavior reminds you that your time with him is dwindling. You are used to him being strong, and you think, "This isn't right. This shouldn't be happening to my dad. He shouldn't be acting this way."

Some of your feelings may result from your awareness of unresolved issues between you and your father. Or maybe you realize that he never responded to you the way you always wanted him to. Now you're facing his diminished capabilities and eventual death, and you fear you will never resolve these painful issues. This fear can spark all kinds of feelings.

Another reason for negative feelings at this time is that your father's decline reminds you that you too will someday grow old, change and die as your father is doing. Your strong emotional reaction to your aging father is your defense against your own aging process.

Your feelings may impinge on some of the necessary decisions you must make concerning your aging father. Whether you feel like it or not, you may need to intervene in a number of ways in his life: where he lives, whether he drives a car or not, how often he gets out to shop or attend church, etc. There are some decisions you must make which are not pleasant, such as whether or not to place your father in a nursing home. But these decisions, and the feelings which accompany them, are all part of the changing of seasons as the old, who raised the young, are now cared for by the young.[5]

When you are at the place of making decisions concerning your father, there are a number of questions to consider which will help you sort through your feelings and inner conflicts.

Am I acting out of guilt or caring?

Am I acting out of reason or panic? out of past hatred or grudges? out of concern for what my father did for me?

Is my decision an act of love?

Am I influenced in this decision by others?

Am I avoiding confronting some of my father's ills and needs because I prefer not to be burdened by his needs?

Do I avoid seeing him because of the pain I feel

when I remember the way he used to be compared to the way he is now?

Is the solution I have arrived at the best for him or simply the cheapest?

If I am placing my father in a care facility, is it best for him, for me or for both of us?

Am I assuming too much responsibility? If so, why?

If I take care of my father alone, what is the cost to my family, my job and my health.

Would I want my children to care for me the way I am caring for my father?[6]

As you become increasingly involved in your aging father's life, don't try to assume all the responsibility by yourself. Ask siblings, other family members or friends to work with you toward responsible decisions concerning your father. It's important to have realistic expectations for your father and for yourself at this time. Involving others will help keep those expectations in perspective.

Relating to Your Aging Father

Relating to your father as he grows older will be difficult whether your relationship with him was healthy and fulfilling or painful and lacking. It's true that life will be more difficult if your experience with him was the latter, but there will be adjustments on your part either way. And if you are the child who lives closest to your father, his care may fall to you. Whether you were the scapegoat, the favorite or the hero in the family, whether or not you have the time, energy, finances or desire, whether or not you feel qualified, you may need to be directly involved in caring for him when he can no longer care for himself.

Some of his problems may present new challenges to

you, and you may resent having to tackle them. But such an experience could be an opportunity for your own personal growth and development. This time in your life may require that you break out of the parent-child relationship in order to see and relate to your father as a person, not just as your father.

It is important that you determine how you want to respond to your aging father, or else you will end up reacting to him based on your feelings or his complaints, helplessness or daily problems. In order to help you understand how you presently respond to your father and help you plan how you want to respond, consider the Ladder of Emotion developed by Carol Flax and Earl Ubell. The eight rungs of the ladder reflect eight different levels of emotion you can experience with your father in any given conversation. Determining your emotional response to your father in advance will help you set boundaries for how you will relate to him and what you will do for him. You can apply the Ladder of Emotion to your father even if he is still middle-aged, strong and healthy. It will prepare you for your relationship with him when he becomes more dependent and demanding:

THE LADDER OF EMOTION

1. I will listen to you.
2. I am interested in what you have to say.
3. I like you and I am interested in what you have to say.
4. I like you and I want to help you.
5. I care for you and I am interested in what you have to say.
6. I care for you and I want to help you.
7. I love you and I am interested in what you have to say.
8. I love you and I want to help you.[7]

The eight different responses on the ladder relate to the way you listen to your father. The first four describe that you are listening primarily for facts, whereas the last four suggest that you are expressing a deeper concern, and perhaps even becoming personally involved. How do you usually respond to your father during a conversation? Why do you respond that way? How do you feel you *should* respond to him? How would you *like* to respond?

Unfortunately, some fathers are difficult to like. They are often angry, obstinate or demanding men who make life anything but pleasant for their children. If you have a father who is difficult to like, you can't disown him; he's still your father. You must decide to relate to him based on your love for him, not your feelings about him.

Over the years it has helped me to view cranky, angry, griping people for what they really are: hurting people or fearful people. When I respond to their true feelings of hurt or fear instead of being taken in or set off by their outer behavior, the relationship is much different. When you look past your father's gruff exterior and identify his inner, often hidden feelings, you will be able to relate to him in a loving, comforting way.

Flax and Ubell go on to describe four different kinds of relationships which can exist between an adult daughter and her father. Which of these represents your present relationship with your father? Which do you want to represent your relationship with him in the future?

1. Minimal relationship. If you have a minimal relationship with your father, you might say, "I want only to talk. I want to be able to speak to my dad; to hear and be heard by him. I want very little or no hostility in our interactions." This type of relationship reflects great emotional distance between you and your father. A minimal relationship probably involves the first four levels of the Emotional Ladder and nothing more. It is a shallow relationship and yet, for some, that's all they can maintain at this time. For others the minimal relationship is a stepping stone to a stronger relationship in time.

If your relationship with your father does not even measure up to the description of a minimal relationship, it has obviously been severely damaged. You talk with your dad, but your involvement in actually helping him is nearly nonexistent. You may avoid calling him to ask for any kind of help or support.

Was there ever a time when your relationship with your father was minimal? Below minimal? If so, what was taking place in his life and your life at that time? Who else contributed to your relationship being minimal? Is this the level of relationship you want with your father at this time in your lives?

2. Moderate relationship. Participants in a moderate relationship say, "I want mutual emotional support. I am willing to give emotional support if needed. I am willing to accept emotional support if offered." All the characteristics of the minimal relationship are present with little or no hostility. Also, there is a greater degree of listening to one another's needs and hurts.

Here are two conversations between a father and his daughter. The first conversation is an example of a relationship which is more minimal than moderate:

> Father: Janice, I just got a phone call. Your favorite cousin, Myra, just died.
>
> Janice: Oh no. I can't believe it. We used to have such a great time together. I'm devastated. I'm going to miss her so much.

Father: If you felt that close to her, why didn't you
   ever call her or get together with her?

Janice: You know how busy I've been with the new
   job, and she lived so far away. But I did call her
   now and then.

Father: You knew she had been sick for awhile, and I
   know she wanted you to come see her. You should
   have . . .

Janice: I told you why I couldn't go see her. You're
   the one with all the time on your hands. Why didn't
   you go see her? Quit blaming me. I'm upset
   enough over losing her.

This was an attacking, not a supportive, conversation.
The adult daughter immediately focused on her own grief
rather than her father's. Let's consider the same conversation from the level of a moderate relationship:

Father: Janice, I just got a phone call. Your favorite
   cousin, Myra, just died.

Janice: Oh no. What a shock. That must have hit you
   hard, Dad. She was your favorite niece.

Father: Yes, she was. I knew she was sick, but this
   was so unexpected.

Janice: You're going to miss her and so am I. We had
   such good times together at the lake.

Father: I think we'll all miss her. I know you were
   close, too. The two of you used to double date
   together years ago.

Janice: It is such a shock. I wish I had spent more
   time with her over the past few years. There are a
   lot of good memories.

Father: It does hurt for both of us.

Notice the difference. The daughter responded to her father and nurtured his feelings. There may be many times when you wish your father would reach out and minister to you first, as Janice did to her father, but it doesn't happen. If there is any nurturing done, you must do it. The older your father becomes, the less capable he will be of meeting your expectations in this area. But you still have the ability to nurture him. Perhaps your example will encourage him to respond in kind.

3. Strong relationship. In a strong relationship, participants say, "I want a mutually helpful relationship. I am willing to provide help if needed. I am willing to accept help if offered." Strong relationships include emotional support, but move on to giving and receiving help. Notice the progression in this emotionally nurturing conversation:

> Father: Everything is so expensive these days. Life was easier years ago.
>
> Daughter: You're finding it rough trying to pay for everything, aren't you?
>
> Father: Yeah. When you're on a fixed income, prices go up but the monthly check stays the same.
>
> Daughter: Are you saying that you need more money to make ends meet?
>
> Father (pausing): I guess I am. But I don't know how to get more money.
>
> Daughter: Is there something specific you need at this time? I would like to know.
>
> Father: Well, I'm hesitant to mention it. I sure don't want to be a burden. But I would like to pick up an extra $25 a week somehow.
>
> Daughter: Would that help you out?

Father: For awhile it would, until the next interest
check comes in. But I don't want to burden you.

Daughter: I don't think it would be a burden. I definitely want to help, and I would feel better knowing
that you have what you need.

Father: I feel better that we have talked about it.
And if you can manage to help, I would appreciate
it—but only until that interest check comes. Is
that agreeable?

Daughter: It sure is.

That was a delicate issue. It was humbling for the
father to admit that he needed financial help. His emphasis
on his interest check was his way of saying that he would
be able to handle his needs in the future, helping him maintain a sense of independence.

4. Ultimate relationship. The strongest relationship is a
combination of the previous three. Those in an ultimate
relationship say, "I want a trusting, loving relationship. I
want to feel safe when I reveal my inner needs, thoughts
and feelings. I want to offer safety for you to reveal your
inner needs, thoughts and feelings. I want and will give
comfort."[8]

Naturally, a relationship of this depth is built over a
period of years. It is achieved by moving through each of
the other levels. Given enough time and effort, even a
strained relationship can grow to become an ultimate relationship. The ultimate relationship reflects the scriptural
model of how we are to love one another (John 13:34),
bear with one another and make allowances for one
another (Eph. 4:2), serve one another (Gal. 5:13), be kind
to one another (Eph. 4:32) and strengthen and build up
one another, just to mention a few.

Instead of viewing your father's old age as a negative period in both his life and yours, see it as a time for growth in you and in your relationship with him. One good way to take advantage of your father's declining years is to capture information and memories from him which would otherwise be lost with his death. Some adult children have gone through family photo albums with their aging parents, encouraging them to share memories from childhood. Some have recorded these sessions on audio or video tape. Experiences like these can be rich for everyone involved. My parents have passed on to me many rolls of home movies which chronicle the last 35 years of my life. I have transferred them to video tape so they can be passed on to others in our family.

When Dad Dies

"When I answered the phone last week, my sister simply said, 'Father is gone,'" Amy told me. "I kept asking her what happened, but all she could say was, 'Father is gone.' Finally I got all the details about his death. Now I really miss him. We had such a good relationship. I was the youngest child, and by the time I came along, Dad had mellowed out. In fact, when all the brothers and sisters got together last week and shared our memories about Dad, I wondered if we were talking about the same man. Our memories about him are so different. I guess I feel fortunate since most of my memories are quite pleasant."

The death of father or mother often revive in adult children the fearful childhood question, "What happens to me when Mother or Father dies?" If this event is yet in the future for you, it will be helpful for you to deal with this reality now. If your father has already died, it may be helpful for you to reflect once again upon the meaning of his death to you. For the Christian daughter who enjoyed a healthy relationship with her believing father, her deep sorrow at his passing will be balanced with the hope of being reunited with him in Christ's presence. The Christian daughter who enjoyed a healthy relationship with an unbelieving father will not only grieve over his death but over the finality of their separation.

Some daughters, whose fathers died suddenly, felt like they were interrupted in the middle of a conversation with no possibility of completing it.

The intensity of a daughter's sense of loss and her ability to cope with her father's death depends on a number of factors. If father and daughter were emotionally close, and most of the loose ends of their relationship were tied up, the pain of separation will be lessened. But if her father dies leaving the unfinished business of many issues unresolved, her pain is intensified. Some daughters, whose fathers died suddenly, felt like they were interrupted in the middle of a conversation with no possibility of completing it.

Your memories of your father are created over all the years you knew him: the simplicity of childhood, the turbulence of adolescence, the maturity of adulthood. I invite you to reflect on a few questions which will help you focus on the highlights of your memories of your father. The questions have been arranged into two sections: the first

260 *Always Daddy's Girl*

for those whose fathers have died and the second for those whose fathers are still living.

If your father has died . . .

1. How often do you think about him?
2. What is your most frequent memory of him?
3. How often do others refer to him?
4. What was the most significant influence your father made on your life?
5. What was unresolved between you and your father when he died?
6. Do you have any regrets or "if onlys" about your relationship with your father?
7. What is your father best remembered for?
8. How has your life been different since he died?

If your father is still living . . .

1. How often do you think about him now?
2. After he is gone, what memories do you want to have about him?
3. How do you feel about your father at this time in your life?
4. What type of relationship do you have with your father at this time: minimal, moderate, strong or ultimate? What kind of relationship would you like to have with him? What is the possibility of developing this relationship?
5. What is your father's most significant influence upon your life at this time?
6. What is unresolved between the two of you at this time?

7. Do you have any regrets or "if onlys" now? What can you do about them now?
8. How do you feel when you think about his eventual death?
9. How will his death affect you? How will you respond?
10. What would you like to talk about with your father before he dies? When will you do it?

Dealing with Regrets

It is not unusual for an adult child to feel a number of regrets when a parent dies. A regret is a sense of remorse or guilt from something you did or said—or neglected to do or say—in your relationship. It is important that you unravel existing feelings of remorse and guilt, and get rid of the "if onlys" you may be carrying around. If your father has died, you may still be experiencing some painful regrets. This section will help you deal with them and dispense with them. If your father is still living, this section may help you prevent the accumulation of regrets which will intensify your sense of loss when he dies.

Here's a suggestion for dealing with your regrets which has been recommended by many counselors in the field of grief recovery. Obtain a family photo album and as many pictures of your father as possible. You will also need writing materials and a period of uninterrupted time—30 minutes to an hour.

Look through the photographs slowly, concentrating on the images of your father and recapturing the memories. Then, as if you were writing a letter to your father, list any regrets you feel about your relationship with him which the photos bring to mind. The process of writing will help you clearly identify your feelings and begin to loosen

the grip these feelings have on you. Also, simply expressing some of your previously unexpressed positive feelings
about your father can be a healing process. There is great
value in completing this exercise whether you have
intense feelings about what you are doing or nothing emotional happens at all. The more specific your "if onlys" are,
the more you will be released from their hold on you.

It is important to remember that you are not doing this
to berate yourself, dwell on your guilt or focus on any
anger or resentment you have toward your father. In an
earlier chapter we discussed the process of forgiving your
father. This exercise will help you forgive yourself and
give up living in the past. Be compassionate toward yourself as you complete the exercise.

In counseling, Pam shared how upset she was at her
father's untimely death a year earlier. We discussed some
of her feelings in depth and Pam came to the place where
she wanted to free herself from the regrets from her past.
Here is the list of regrets she shared with me:

Dear Dad,

I regret that I didn't spend much time with you
the last few months.

I regret that I never really got to know what you
were like as a person.

I regret that we couldn't say good-bye to each
other.

I regret the times I did things that hurt you so
much.

I regret that I didn't marry earlier so that you
could walk me down the aisle and give me away.

I regret that I can no longer call up and say, "Hi
Dad."

I regret that I won't be able to rely upon your wisdom and experience in my job.

Some of you will list only two or three regrets. Others will list 15 or more. It doesn't matter how many you list. Keep writing until you can't think of anything more.

Most people find it helpful to use the empty chair technique to complete the process. Sit down opposite an empty chair and read your list of regrets aloud to the chair as if your father was sitting there. Sometimes it helps to put a trusted friend or a counselor in the empty chair and read to him or her.

It may help you to remember that you probably aren't the only person in your father-daughter relationship who has regrets. Your father undoubtedly carries—or carried to his grave—his own list of regrets. Very few of us say or do all that we intend or wish we had done. That's why we must be thankful for the gift of forgiveness that God has given us for ourselves and others.

Death is not the most popular or pleasant topic for discussion in our society. We would prefer to ignore its presence until we are personally confronted by it. We subconsciously cling to the myth that death happens to other people, but not to our families. It's only when death strikes close to home that we realize, "Yes, it's also waiting for my family members and for me."

Let me close this chapter with one last hopeful thought. For the Christian, dying is a home-going, a reunion of believers. David Morley describes our last journey beautifully:

"What a joyous moment that will be, when he will be reunited with all of his loved ones who have gone on before! When, once more, the lines of communication will be reestablished, the old voices heard again, and the deathly silence at last broken forever—no more good-byes, no more quick slipping away of loved ones into the mysterious enigma of death."

The most glorious anticipation of the Christian is that, at the time of death, he will come face to face with his blessed Lord, his wonderful, patient Redeemer, who all of those years continued to love him in spite of the countless times the man ignored Him and went his willful way. We will not be encountering a stranger, but the best and most intimate friend that we have ever had. When we think of death as a time of revelation and reunion, we immediately remove its venom. We can say with the Apostle Paul, "O death, where is thy sting? O grave, where is thy victory?" (1 Corinthians 15:55).[9]

Notes

1. From *Making Peace with Your Parents*, by Harold H. Bloomfield, M.D. and Leonard Felder, Ph.D. Copyright © 1983 by Bloomfield Productions, Inc. Reprinted by permission of Random House, Inc.
2. Leopold Bellak, *The Best Years of Your Life* (NY: Atheneum, 1975), p. 5. Reprinted by permission of Curtis Brown, Ltd.
3. *Behavior Today Newsletter* (November 7, 1988), adapted from p. 3.
4. Bellak, *The Best Years of Your Life*, p. 24.
5. Howard Halpern, *Cutting Loose* (NY: Bantam Books, 1977), adapted from pp. 198-199.
6. Ibid., adapted from p. 198.
7. Carol Flax and Earl Ubell, *Mother, Father, You* (Ridgefield, CT: Wyden Books, 1989), p. 184.
8. Ibid., adapted from p. 192-201.
9. David C. Morley, *Halfway Up the Mountain* (Old Tappan, NJ: Fleming H. Revell, 1979), pp. 77-78. Used by permission.

FOURTEEN

A Letter to Fathers of Daughters

I am the father of a daughter. As I write this, it has been a 28-year journey of fathering, more than a quarter of a century filled with a rich array of experiences with Sheryl. Like most men, I wasn't really prepared to be a father. No one sat me down and equipped me with insights for my role. I guess I was just supposed to know how to be a father. But I soon discovered that I didn't know enough, and I was a little frightened. Most of us men don't talk openly about our fears. It probably would help us if we did, especially our fears about fathering.

How did you feel when you first held your daughter: apprehensive? hesitant? awestruck? I remember wondering, "How do I hold her? I don't want to drop her. What if she cries? What if she doesn't stop crying?" Many new fathers react this way. Other men prepare for their role by attending classes, reading books, serving in the church nursery and interacting with other fathers. If you were a confident father right from the start, you were fortunate.

The Joys of Fathering

A daughter can bring great joy into a father's life. In her first days in school she brought you joy by sharing her exciting discoveries. As an adult she brings great joy when she concludes her phone conversations with the words, "I love you, Dad." Recently I found a note from Sheryl in my dresser drawer which simply said, "Thanks for being my Daddy." Those five simple words filled my heart with joy.

Have you reflected on all the joy-filled memories your daughter has brought into your life? Have you ever told her about them? Just writing this letter to you has flooded my mind with a wide range of wonderful memories from being Sheryl's father. Watching her as a five-year-old bait a hook, cast it out and reel in her own fish brought me joy. Hiking with her along many streams and fishing together as she was growing up brought me joy.

I have a happy memory of playing a duet with Sheryl for her final piano recital when she was in high school. It was supposed to be a serious recital. But to the piano teacher's chagrin, our sheet music fell off the piano and Sheryl and I got the giggles. Actually, I'm glad it happened. The event is even more vivid in my memory because of it.

Listening to Sheryl describe how she invited Jesus Christ into her life brought me great joy. Years later, my joy was almost uncontainable when I walked forward with her in church as she rededicated her life to Christ after going her own way. Seeing her grow spiritually in the following months was a delight to me. And just recently, hearing her tell us about some of her personal prayer experiences brought me joy.

Sheryl's wedding in 1988 was another joyous event for me for two particular reasons. Naturally, the wedding day itself was a high point in my life. But prior to her wedding day, Sheryl came to talk to Joyce and me about her brother, Matthew, who was 22 years old at the time. Matthew is profoundly mentally retarded, having lived out of our home since he was 11. "I know Matthew won't be able to come to the ceremony," Sheryl said. "But I would still like him to be a part of my wedding. The next time he is home for a visit, could we rent a tuxedo for him so he and I can be photographed together?"

Needless to say, her request brought a deep sense of joy to her mother and me. Due to many factors, we were unable to fulfill her request, but that was all right. Sheryl's thoughtful offer was very meaningful to us and it remains a precious memory.

I have hundreds of happy memories like these, and you will probably have them too. Each one is a gift which will enrich your life.

Fathering Can Be Frustrating

As fathers, we also experience frustration, disappointment, upset and grief as we raise our daughters. Many of these feelings result from our unfulfilled expectations. Your expectations for your daughter will not all be fulfilled, even though many of them are realistic and positive. As much as you may want to, you cannot completely determine what your daughter will become, accomplish or believe. And if your expectations are unrealistic, your disappointment will be even deeper.

You may want your daughter to obtain a master's degree and enter a professional vocation. But she may not be interested in academics and may choose another career path. Perhaps you're hoping she will marry young and present you with several grandchildren. But she may prefer to establish a career, marry late and forego children altogether. You expect her to marry a college graduate, but her husband may have just barely finished high school. You want her to have lots of friends and be very popular, but she may prefer the quiet life.

I had high hopes for Sheryl academically. There were two reasons for my expectations—reasons I understand much better now than I did then. First, when I realized that Matthew would never develop mentally beyond a two-year-old, I was especially hopeful that Sheryl would be studious and complete college. Second, since I had completed college and two graduate programs, a total of eight years, I hoped my daughter would follow in my academic footsteps.

But as Sheryl progressed through high school, I could see that she had other interests. After completing one year of college she became a licensed manicurist and went to work in a beauty salon. Her career choice wasn't what I would have chosen for her, but that was all right. Joyce and I have always encouraged her to do her best in whatever she tackled, and Sheryl began to excel in her field. She applied her God-given artistic talent to her work as a manicurist by doing nail art—painting miniature scenes on the nails of her customers. Her skill developed to the point that she won several national competitions, and she has instructed many others in this art.

Today her artistic gifts are taking her in an exciting new direction. She has developed a line of hand-painted earrings which are catching on around the country. Sheryl's career is much more fulfilling to her—and, as such, fulfilling to her mother and me—than my choices for her would have been. She enjoys doing things a little bit differently and creating her own business. And in that way she *is* like her father!

There are also times of heartache in fathering. I'll never forget the day 21-year-old Sheryl walked into my office and dropped a bombshell on me. She calmly told me that she understood the values her mother and I had lived by and taught her, but she had decided to take a different direction. I was devastated. Every morning for three months I grieved for her, weeping as I rode my exercise bicycle and listened to a Dennis Agajanian tune titled, "Rebel to the Wrong." For four years we prayed for her, loved her, believed for her and waited for her to turn back to the Lord. Those were difficult, painful years.

Then one Sunday morning, the joyous occasion of her rededication to Christ that I mentioned earlier occurred. Sheryl and I were sitting together in church. During the invitation at the close of the service, she turned to me and said, "Daddy, will you walk up there with me?" I tearfully escorted her to the altar and had the privilege of seeing her recommit her life to Jesus Christ. Later Sheryl said, "Daddy, I was doing fine emotionally until I looked at you and saw that you were losing it." We both laughed at her comment, realizing that our tears were tears of joy. I'm thankful that God can even turn our experiences of heartache with our daughters into occasions for great joy. The parable of the prodigal son in Luke 15 means so much more to me now.

How well do you handle your disappointments? When you are frustrated or disappointed, do you become angry over your hurts or depressed over your losses? It's important that you express your feelings in a healthy, constructive way. Burying your disappointments or avoiding the issues will only delay your opportunity to adjust your hopes and dreams for your daughter.

Ten Tips for Fathering Daughters

I'm not sure how you got hold of this book. It's really written to help daughters understand and deal with their relationships with their fathers. Perhaps your wife, your daughter or a friend is reading it and you found it lying on the coffee table, or it mysteriously appeared on your night stand. Or maybe you bought it yourself in order to better understand your daughter and her relationship to you. It doesn't matter to me how you happened to pick it up, I'm just glad you did.

If your daughter has adopted unwholesome values, seek to influence her through your love, acceptance, prayer and positive example instead of sermons and ultimatums.

Although the previous 13 chapters are directed to your adult daughter, you see from the title that this chapter is for you. I want to share with you ten vital tips by which you can improve your relationship with your daughter. Each one of these tips relates to information I have already shared with your daughter in previous chapters. I have included the chapter numbers in each heading in case you want to read a little more about each topic.

What does your daughter think about you at this time in your life? How does your daughter feel about you? Do you know? In chapter 1 you will find the responses of several daughters who were asked to describe the positive and negative qualities of their fathers. Read their comments and, for each one, ask yourself, "Would my daughter say this about me? Why or why not?" You may want to ask your daughter to list the positive and negative qualities she sees in you. It could be a threatening experience for you, but it will also be enlightening.

Whether your daughter is a child, an adolescent or an adult, you still have an opportunity to influence her life for the better. It is my prayer that you will take these tips to heart and look for practical ways to apply them to your relationship with your little girl.

1. Accept her values (see chapter 1). No matter how old your daughter may be, you have influenced—and are presently influencing—her values and beliefs. She has accepted some of your values for her life, modified others and discarded still others. It is important that you affirm your daughter by accepting her values. She isn't supposed to be a photocopy of you. As someone has said, "If two people are exactly the same, one of them isn't necessary." If your daughter has adopted unwholesome values, seek to influence her through your love, acceptance, prayer and positive example instead of sermons and ultimatums.

Do you know what your daughter's values are? In chapter 1, I asked daughters reading this book to reflect on how their fathers have influenced their values on 14 different issues. First they recorded what their fathers said about each issue. Then daughters recorded what they believe now. Recently I asked Sheryl to complete the exercise, and she asked me to read over her responses. Our discussion about values was highly enjoyable and informative for both of us. Here are a few of her responses:

Money

My dad always said, "When you have an impulse to buy something, wait awhile and see if you still want it."
What I believe now is, "The same, but I only practice it 50 percent of the time."

Women

My dad always said, "Women can do anything they set their minds on."
What I believe now is, "The same."

School

My dad always said, "Do the best you can, like the time you got a *C* in math instead of a *D*."
What I believe now is, "The same."

Self-esteem

My dad always said, "Don't be so hard on yourself."
What I believe now is, "There is good in everyone; focus on your good points and work on your weak points."

Your daughter may have already completed this exercise in chapter 1, or she may be planning to complete it. Hopefully she will want to share her responses with you. Before she does, however, read through the 14 issues and try to remember what values you communicated to your daughter regarding them. Then prepare yourself for an interesting discussion!

2. Encourage her femininity and sexuality (see chapter 2). As a father, you are helping your daughter develop her perceptions of men as well as her expectations for the men in her life. You are influencing her attitudes, beliefs, hopes and dreams about men, and her responses to men. That's quite a responsibility.

You are also a vital influence on the development of your daughter's femininity and sexuality. You are the first man in her life, and she needs you to approve the expressions of her feminine charms. Many men leave it up to their wives to say, "You know, your father really loves you and is proud of you. You ought to hear how he talks about you when he's with our friends." Tell her directly that you love her, appreciate her and value her as a woman. Smile or wink at her when she bats her eyelashes at you. Tell her how lovely and attractive she is in her new dress or hair style. When a father fails to acknowledge his daughter's femininity, she is stunted and incomplete in her development. Too often she is left to discover her femininity for herself, often with tragic results in her relationships with the men in her life.

Don't be threatened by her developing sexuality. Some fathers are so uncomfortable with the sexual development of their daughters that they ridicule them, ignore them or reject them instead of affirm them. Your daughter's sexuality can be encouraged or retarded by your responses to her. A long-time friend of mine, Dr. Norman Wakefield, shared his thoughts and experience on this issue in his book, *The Dad Difference*:

> Since our society has become aware of great sexual abuse among the masses, men are more fearful than ever of touching children (we are speaking here of healthy, positive physical contact). Yet, if dads do not

embrace their sons and daughters and thus show positive affection for them, their distancing themselves will send a negative message to their children.

I recall when my oldest daughter, Amy, reached puberty. I sensed a tendency within myself to draw back and be more reserved. At the same time I realized that Amy still needed my warmth and affection, perhaps more than ever. I decided to follow what I knew was in Amy's best interest, and not allow my uncomfortable feelings to dictate my behavior. I continued giving her hugs and expressing affection as I had before. The close relationship I now enjoy with Amy in her adulthood makes me thankful I made that choice.

One young adult woman recently shared with me how her dad seemed to suddenly quit hugging her when she began to blossom into womanhood. "As a typical egocentric teenager," she told me, "I assumed something was wrong with me. It never occurred to me that my own dad would be uncomfortable because of my emerging sexuality." We need to put dads at ease and encourage them to continue giving what their daughters are indicating they need—a touch on the arm, an arm around the shoulder, a warm hug—to affirm their love and devotion.[1]

Your daughter needs to hear what you believe and feel about sex. She needs your perceptions of how men think and respond sexually. She needs to know that you and your wife have a healthy sexual relationship, and that you revere sex as a gift from God. Creating a positive atmosphere about sex and sexuality will help her share her thoughts about herself, her femininity, her sexuality and men.

3. Encourage her potential (see chapter 2). Challenge and encourage your daughter to be all that she can be. Let her know that she is a child of the King, our Lord Jesus Christ. It will help her feel special. Give her an expanded view of her potential, and not a limited view, as mentioned in chapter 2.

Your work and your career are important to you, as they are to most men. What your daughter sees you do and hears you say about your work will impact her perspective of her potential. Be sure to emphasize to her to do her best, rather than overemphasize winning or achieving. She needs to learn from you about the enjoyment and fulfillment of doing things well, as well as delivering the end product.

Your daughter needs to see that work is not your first priority in life. If you let your work determine who you are and how you feel about yourself, she may follow suit. You are more than what you do or produce on the job, and so is she. Help her understand through your example that her vocation is only an expression of who she is, not the determining factor of her identity.

4. Let her see your emotional side (see chapter 3). Many daughters go through life not really knowing their fathers because men so often withhold warmth, tenderness and intimacy from their wives and children. Men tend to hide behind the armor plating of their anger, which is often the only emotion their families see. Balance your emotional expression to include the full range of positive feelings.

In chapter 3 you will find a number of responses from women who were asked, "What emotions does your father express and how does he express them?" Read their answers, then ask yourself, "How would my daughter answer that question?" Would she say you are balanced in your emotional expressions? Why or why not?

5. Take time to communicate with her (see chapter 3).
Sometimes, when we men think we have talked enough
about a topic, the women in our lives are just getting
started. Allow plenty of time for you and your daughter to
talk things out to her satisfaction. Listen carefully to what
she is saying and even more carefully to the message
behind her words. Treat every opportunity to spend time
with your daughter as a unique gift from God that will
never occur in the same way again. And allow the time you
spend with her to be a gift to her from you.

Your daughter's timing for being together may not
always coincide with your timing. When Sheryl was 12
years old, she came home from a piano lesson with a new
piece of music: "Sunrise, Sunset" from *Fiddler on the
Roof.* "Daddy, will you play this for me?" she asked. I set
aside the book I was reading, rose from my comfortable
recliner, sat down at the piano and played the piece several times, much to Sheryl's delight.

After dinner I again settled into my chair to relax and
read. "Daddy, will you play it again?" Sheryl begged. My
first response, which I did not verbalize aloud, was,
"Sheryl, I've already played 'Sunrise, Sunset' enough for
one day. I want to read. Play it yourself this time." But I
think I heard the Lord saying to me, "You're not too busy.
Take time for Sheryl." So I left my chair again and began
playing for her. Soon Joyce and Sheryl were standing
behind me singing the words to the beautiful tune.

Then it hit me: The lyrics describe a father's feelings
about his little girl becoming a young woman. I suddenly
realized that the words expressed some of my feelings
about seeing Sheryl grow up. I played the song several
times as Joyce and Sheryl sang. It became a very impor-

tant and special time in my relationship with Sheryl—and it cost me less than 15 minutes. But I came so close to missing it by saying, "I'm too busy."

One meaningful method for spending time with your daughter is to complete the Father Interview in chapter 3. If she has not already requested you to answer the questions, perhaps you could suggest the activity to her.

6. Involve yourself in her life (see chapters 4, 5 and 6). Chapters 4, 5 and 6 describe the tragic consequences in a daughter's life when her father abandons her either through death, desertion or divorce, or through noninvolvement while remaining in the home. The daughter who was emotionally or physically abandoned by her father will have difficulty trusting other men. Her unresolved anger will affect her relationships with men. She may fear intimacy because the first man she ever loved—her father—broke her heart by leaving her in some way. She needs opportunity to deal with her anger.

Many women today grew up with phantom fathers, men who are physically present but emotionally absent and uninvolved in the lives of their daughters. The phantom father is usually a devoted provider, committed to demonstrating his love to his family by giving them a good life. Working 10 to 15 hours a day, six days a week, he has little time to spend getting close to his family. He lives under the same roof with his daughter, and they talk, but they don't really communicate. Many daughters who try to get their phantom fathers involved in their lives end up feeling responsible for his apathy.

If you remain actively involved with your daughter, you won't run the risk of becoming a phantom father. Spend time with her talking, working and playing. Schedule special father-daughter "dates" together. Invite her to share with you her thoughts, feelings and dreams, and share yours with her.

7. Give her space to grow (see chapter 7). Though many fathers abandon their daughters through uninvolvement, other fathers create an opposite but equally hurtful problem by being overinvolved in the lives of their daughters. A woman may grow up and leave her father's home only to find that he still tells her what to do and where to go. I hear these women complain in the counseling office, "I'm 33 years old and married with children of my own, but I still can't get my father out of my life! He still treats me like a helpless little girl—which I'm not."

The father who is overinvolved in his daughter's life reinforces her sense of helplessness and her dependency on him. Instead, he should be encouraging her capabilities and independence, preparing her for life on her own. If you dominate your daughter and don't give her room to grow and develop, she will be ill-equipped to function as an adult.

8. Give her a healthy family (see chapters 8 and 9). Chapter 8 contrasts the positive characteristics of a healthy family with the negative characteristics of a dysfunctional family. Chapter 9 continues the theme by describing the dysfunctional roles individuals often adopt in response to their upbringing in dysfunctional families. Reading these chapters will help you and your family in at least three ways. First, the descriptions will help you evaluate your present family relationships and determine if you are headed in the right direction. Second, this information will help you understand your wife's background and family, which will give you clearer insight into her thoughts, feelings and responses. Third, investigating the traits of healthy and dysfunctional families will help you better understand your own family background and how it influences your relationship with your daughter today.

9. Nurture her self-esteem and identity (see chapter 10). In chapter 10, you will find many insights into how you can encourage the development of your daughter's self-esteem and identity. I want to suggest one additional way here: blessing your daughter. In the Old Testament you will find several occasions where fathers blessed their children. These blessings signified acceptance, which is foundational to building self-esteem. Blessing your daughter will bolster her self-image and help solidify her unique identity.

Recognize your daughter as a very special person and communicate her specialness through your words. Treat her in ways which show that you treasure her as a wonderful gift.

In their book, *The Blessing*, Gary Smalley and John Trent suggest five elements which constitute a blessing. The first is *meaningful touch*. Studies show that loving touches greatly enhance physical and emotional health. Hugging your daughter, placing your hand on her head and gently squeezing her shoulder convey love and acceptance to her and create a close bond between you.

Second, blessing may be bestowed through *spoken words*—words of love, affirmation and acceptance. Bless your daughter with kind words every day. Watch her closely for things to compliment her about, especially things you have taken for granted. Plan ahead and make a list of positive, encouraging words you want to say to her.

The third element of a blessing is *expressing high value* to your daughter. Recognize your daughter as a very special person and communicate her specialness through your words. Treat her in ways which show that you treasure her as a wonderful gift. Let her know that you believe in her. Let her know that you see her as a person with great potential, even when she isn't living up to your standards. She will rise to the challenge of meeting your positive expectations for her.

The fourth element of a blessing is *picturing a special future* for your daughter. What do you communicate to your daughter about her future? Does she feel hopeful or discouraged because of your messages to her about what lies ahead? Does she hear you saying, "I don't know if you have what it takes" or "Go for it, Sweetheart; you can do it!"

Isaac blessed Jacob with hopeful words about his future (Gen. 27:28-29). Jesus blessed us with words of promise concerning our future with Him (John 14:2-3). You will encourage and guide your daughter through your positive words about what she is becoming and what she will accomplish.

The final element of a blessing is an *active commitment* from you to do everything you can to help her fulfill her potential. Your commitment includes giving your time and resources. It means disciplining yourself to grow and develop in order to be a more effective model and guide. Your commitment involves praying for your daughter daily and sharing God's Word with her through what you say and how you live your life. And it requires that you understand—and help her develop—her uniqueness instead of forcing her into your mold for what she should be. Proverbs 22:6 says: "Train up a child in the way he should go [and in keeping with his individual gift or bent], and when he is old he will not depart from it" (*AMP*). Your daughter is different from anyone else. Help her discover and channel her "individual gift or bent" to achieve her potential and reflect the presence of Jesus Christ in her life.[2]

10. Release her to her husband (see chapters 11 and 12). One of the major transitions in a father's life is releasing his single daughter to become his married daughter. He has been the number one man in her life since she was born. But for most daughters, eventually another man comes along who will take top billing from her father. At that point you must release her into the care and protection of the husband God has given her. This transition took place for Sheryl and me in 1988.

During more than 25 years of premarital counseling, I have requested that the parents of the engaged couple write a letter to their prospective son- or daughter-in-law welcoming him or her into their family. I have heard hundreds of these letters read in my office. For years I looked forward to writing such a letter to Sheryl's future husband. I was glad when Bill and Sheryl's counselor, who is a good friend of mine, requested that Joyce and I write a letter of welcome to Bill, which we did.

But we also wanted to write a letter to Sheryl. We wanted to express to her in a special way how we loved her and how happy we were for her future with Bill. It was our way of releasing her to the man God had brought into her life.

Following the counselor's instructions, I mailed our

letter for Bill to the counselor and included our letter to Sheryl. When their counseling session came, he shared the letters with each of them from their future parents-in-law. Then he said to Sheryl, "There is an additional letter here for you, Sheryl, from your parents. But instead of giving this to you to read, let me suggest that you take it home and ask your father to read it to you."

When she came home with that information, I was surprised. Yet, knowing her counselor as I do, it shouldn't have surprised me that he would suggest that I read the letter.

Interestingly, I waited for three days before we all sat down together and I read Sheryl this letter from Joyce and me. I am so glad that we were asked to do so. Finally the evening arrived when we sat down with Bill, Sheryl, Bill's parents and the counselor to read our letters. It was such a special time for me to read our letter to Sheryl. With her permission, I want to share it with you:

Dear Sheryl,

You probably didn't expect to receive a letter from us at this time, but we have always wanted to write a letter to our about-to-be-married daughter. And that time is here—finally!

For years we have prayed for your choice of the man with whom you will spend the rest of your life. Patience does have its rewards, doesn't it?

Sheryl, our desire for you is that you have a marriage which is fulfilling, satisfying and glorifying to God. You, as a woman, have so much to offer. You have God-given talents and abilities which, with each year of your life, emerge more and more. You have a sensitivity and love to give Bill which will enhance your marriage.

We know there are times when you get down on yourself and feel discouraged. Never give up on yourself. God never has, nor will, and we never have, nor will. Treat yourself with the respect that God has for you. Allow Him to enable you to continue to develop now as a married woman. Jesus Christ has started a new work in you and He will bring it to completion.

Sheryl, you have brought so much delight and joy into our lives, and we thank God that you have been our daughter for all these years. We have all grown together through learning to accept one another and through some difficult times of hurt and pain. That is life! But because of Jesus Christ, we all learn through those hard times.

We look forward to becoming parents of a married daughter. Mrs. Bill Macualey: doesn't that have a great sound!

Sheryl, thank you for how you have enriched our lives. Thank you for who you are.

> We love you,
> Mom and Dad

Whether your daughter is married yet or not, I suggest that you write a letter to her. Share your feelings about her, encourage her and bless her. Then arrange a time when you can read the letter to her in person. You will find that your relationship with her will become even closer.

Notes

1. Josh McDowell and Norman Wakefield, *The Dad Difference* (San Bernardino, CA: Here's Life Publishers, 1989), pp. 57-58.
2. Gary Smalley and John Trent, *The Blessing* (Nashville, TN: Thomas Nelson Publishers, 1986), adapted from numerous chapters.